## THE DEATH PENALTY FOR

# KARL MARX

ION PAVEL PUIU

Copyright © 2021 by Ion Pavel Puiu.

All rights reserved. No part of this publication may be reproduced, distributed, or transmitted in any form or by any means, including photocopying, recording, or other electronic or mechanical methods, without the prior written permission of the author, except in the case of brief quotations embodied in critical reviews and certain other noncommercial uses permitted by copyright law.

Printed in the United States of America.

Library of Congress Control Number: 2020903097

| ISBN | Paperback | 978-1-68536-795-4 |
|---|---|---|
|  | eBook | 978-1-68536-902-6 |

**Westwood Books Publishing LLC**
Atlanta Financial Center
3343 Peachtree Rd NE Ste 145-725
Atlanta, GA 30326

www.westwoodbookspublishing.com

# CONTENTS

Prologue . . . . . . . . . . . . . . . . . . . . . . . . . . . . . . . . . . . . . . . . . . . . . v

Chapter 1:  Fear . . . . . . . . . . . . . . . . . . . . . . . . . . . . . . . . . . . . . . 1
Chapter 2:  My Friend Bill . . . . . . . . . . . . . . . . . . . . . . . . . . . . . 6
Chapter 3:  Dick Now . . . . . . . . . . . . . . . . . . . . . . . . . . . . . . . . 13
Chapter 4:  Mr. Jack . . . . . . . . . . . . . . . . . . . . . . . . . . . . . . . . . 18
Chapter 5:  My Good, Beloved Father . . . . . . . . . . . . . . . . . . . 23
Chapter 6:  Dick's Predicament . . . . . . . . . . . . . . . . . . . . . . . . 28
Chapter 7:  Gary Explained It Well . . . . . . . . . . . . . . . . . . . . . 33
Chapter 8:  Dick and His World . . . . . . . . . . . . . . . . . . . . . . . 44
Chapter 9:  Dick's Philosophy . . . . . . . . . . . . . . . . . . . . . . . . . 49
Chapter 10: The Funeral . . . . . . . . . . . . . . . . . . . . . . . . . . . . . 54
Chapter 11: Talking to Mr. Glenn . . . . . . . . . . . . . . . . . . . . . . 60
Chapter 12: Eric . . . . . . . . . . . . . . . . . . . . . . . . . . . . . . . . . . . . 74
Chapter 13: Bill and Mark . . . . . . . . . . . . . . . . . . . . . . . . . . . 78
Chapter 14: Eric and Surveillance . . . . . . . . . . . . . . . . . . . . . 102
Chapter 15: Jealous Dick . . . . . . . . . . . . . . . . . . . . . . . . . . . 106
Chapter 16: New Details . . . . . . . . . . . . . . . . . . . . . . . . . . . . 115
Chapter 17: The Rape . . . . . . . . . . . . . . . . . . . . . . . . . . . . . . 124
Chapter 18: In Jail . . . . . . . . . . . . . . . . . . . . . . . . . . . . . . . . . 133
Chapter 19: Trial Time . . . . . . . . . . . . . . . . . . . . . . . . . . . . . 138
Chapter 20: Jane Marries . . . . . . . . . . . . . . . . . . . . . . . . . . . 143
Chapter 21: Dick, Johnny Green Lee, and Eric . . . . . . . . . . . 156
Chapter 22: Mr. Jason . . . . . . . . . . . . . . . . . . . . . . . . . . . . . . 164

Chapter 23: Bill Knows a Lot ........................170
Chapter 24: Jenny Is on to Ping Kong .................182
Chapter 25: The Repair Shop........................189
Chapter 26: Bill Meets Mr. Glenn Again ................194
Chapter 27: Jimmy, Mr. Jason, and Karl Marx ............202
Chapter 28: Jimmy, Roger, and Court for Karl Marx ........220

Epilogue ......................................261

# PROLOGUE

This book is an expression of hope to bring together people around the world.

To help a mother understand and feel the drama of an abandoned child.

To help a father stop the suffering of an innocent who would be very happy to say, "My dear daddy."

Killings caused by boredom, religion, or hatred must cease.

They bring too much torment and drama.

And those who have access to power should know that what they have is not forever, and fast, very fast it goes away.

Forcing time or forgetting that you are nothing else than a passerby may make you think that you deserve everything, that you can do whatever you want, and that overnight you have become God of men.

It is good to help in all honesty, not lying, and to stop the corruption which has become too huge and is conquering wider and wider areas.

The Lord gives you chances.

You have to choose and to create.

Enmity, revenge, hatred, and crime banish them out of your house.

Put instead love, respect for the truth, and honest work.

Always built, never demolish.
Finally, life is so right.
History puts everyone in the place they deserve.

**Puiu Ion Pavel**

# CHAPTER 1

# FEAR

My mother used to come to my bedroom to remind me we had to go out of the city as fast as possible. I could hear the radio in the kitchen, and my four-year-old younger brother would come to play in my bed.

Today everything was different.

This Sunday morning, an unexpected silence descended on our house. No music in the kitchen and no noise in the entire house.

Everything was quiet.

The clock was 8:36 a.m., and I could feel a strange sensation creeping into my heart.

Yesterday my father said, "Tomorrow get ready to go together to the park and prepare all that's needed. We'll start around 9:00 a.m., so be ready and help your mother put everything in the car. Also take care of George because he is so young."

I said, "Sure, no problem." And then Dad kissed me and flicked my nose. I was so happy to see how much Mom and Dad loved each other.

Mom was very proud when dad put on his policeman uniform. And she would arrange his uniform and kissed him before he got into the car.

We, the two sons, would run around them and were so happy for their love. I had never seen my mom and dad have a fight. Our life was so happy, and I felt a great responsibility to take care of George.

I threw my pajamas on the bed, and I ran to the kitchen frightened and apprehensive, but Mom was not there.

I went to my parents' bedroom, and there was nobody there. Their bed was untouched. I started to call George, but he was not in the house either. I ran out to the garden, and there was nobody there too.

I was desperate. What was going on with me and my family? What could it be? What should I do?

Where should I go to find out, and whom should I ask?

A familiar voice called my name, "Dan! Dan! Dan!"

It was our neighbor across the road, Mrs. Hamilton. She was a very nice lady and a great cook. Her son, Scott, was a good friend of mine. We used to play and go to many places together, and we were also classmates.

Scott taught me lots of things. He was very tall and extremely slim, as if he didn't eat anything ever. I'd never heard noise in their house.

Scott loved his parents very much, and he helped them a lot. I'd often seen him coming back home with bags from the grocery store.

The Hamiltons were originally from Louisiana.

Far, far away.

They were a black family.

One day, Scott showed me an old book with yellowed pages. He wouldn't let me touch it or leaf through it.

He promised that one day he would lend it to me, but only for a short time, a very short time.

Scott always needed to sit down and rest.

With him playing was short. He would say, "Let's stop for a while. I'm tired. Let me just catch my breath."

Mrs. Hamilton petted me on the head and tried to say something in a soft voice.

She stopped. She didn't say anything. I saw tears in her eyes.

She asked me to come inside and gave me a treat. I didn't want to, and I couldn't in the state of desperation I was.

Then Mrs. Hamilton went back inside the house without saying anything.

I remember one very long and very cold winter, when I was coming home, I saw Mrs. Hamilton going back inside their house.

I asked her, "What's up with Scott?"

Very agitated and with tears in her eyes, she replied, "Scott is a bit sick. He's got a fever. I gotta take him to the doctor today. We've got an appointment."

I said, "He didn't come to school today, and I wanted to give him the homework."

A little disconcerted, she said, "Homework! What homework? Not now." And then she added, "Oh, yeah, sure."

She had a bewildered look on her face.

Next day, I didn't see Scott in class, and I was surprised.

On my way home, I crossed the street to their house to talk to Scott as I always did.

I rang and rang the bell, and nobody answered. After that, I tried the door, and it was unlocked.

But there was nobody in the house.

I went back home, telling myself that they were probably out running some errands. I started working on my homework, but I didn't go too far. I was really worried.

What was going on with Scott and his family? I felt something strange was going on. I'd find out more tomorrow.

I started playing with George and soon forgot about everything.

George was my younger brother, and he liked nothing better than play with me all day long until the evening came and he fell asleep on the couch. Usually Mom would take him in her arms and put him to bed. She would slowly undress him so as not to wake him up and kiss him from head to toe.

Around nine thirty that night, when we were getting ready to go to bed, somebody knocked on our door. My mother went to the door to see who it was.

Dad said, "Let me get it. It must be for me someone from work." And he headed to the door saying, "Usually somebody calls ahead so I'm ready when the car comes to get me. Who knows, maybe it's an emergency."

Mrs. Hamilton came in. She could hardly stand up. She said in a heartrending voice, "Scott, my good son, is in the hospital morgue. He died so fast."

With tears in her eyes, my mom said, "What? It can't be! Why? And so fast just in a couple of days? It can't be! God, why did you take him, such a good child?"

Choking with pain, Mrs. Hamilton said, "He had black people's disease in his blood, something with the red blood cells. The doctor told us to be prepared since he was five years old. Oh my, his life has been too short."

And tears of sorrow started rolling down her cheeks. I was disturbed by what I'd heard.

My mom and dad talked the whole night. Mrs. Hamilton was very distressed and in lots of pain.

I'm pretty sure they didn't take Scott to the funeral home. They kept him at home for a few days.

I would see people going into Mrs. Hamilton's home from time to time.

And then the day of interment came.

In the cemetery, there were a few families, and it was damn cold. Everything was solid frozen. They lowered Scott in the grave. The whole thing was fast. They were some sort of Baptists.

How sad life can be. At night in bed, I tried to remember Scott.

But I eventually fell asleep.

After Mrs. Hamilton left, I felt overwhelmed by an immense fear. I sensed that even bigger troubles were coming that would brutally invade our quiet life.

I just knew.

There was something strange around me. I felt small and helpless. Nothing could chase my fears away.

I could feel danger just like animals feel death closing in. It was new sensation.

Not for second did I think that very soon, too soon, it would befall on my family, a family so happy until then.

# CHAPTER 2

# MY FRIEND BILL

Sometimes Dad invited Bill to our home.

He was a bit older than me, whose father was also a cop and who had been murdered in the street by a group of drug dealers.

He had received an order to go there and chase them away, but he was by himself and easy be eliminated.

He was shot in the head and then slashed with the knives to make his face unrecognizable. He was found a few hours later in a plastic bag under the bridge.

Bill loved his parents very much. He was well behaved and impressed by his dad.

He was fascinated by his dad's courage and spirit of justice.

He always thought that his dad knew everything and could do the bravest things.

Going to dangerous places in the middle of the night and saving people from great tragedies was fascinating. From his dad, he learned about hard-to-imagine situations, and he was so proud of his dad, who was able to solve them all on the spot.

Bill used to come visit us on Sundays and had long talks with Dad. I don't know what they discussed, but he was delighted.

I liked to be with him, although he didn't like to play too much.

He was preparing to go to college, and Dad used to give him a lot of advice.

My dad was like a real father for him. I think he cared about Bill because he always helped him with advice, gave him some money, and tried to lighten his life, which was so hard for him.

Once I was surprised. I didn't understand, but I didn't tell anyone.

When I stepped into the living room, Bill was crying out loud with his face buried in dad's cop uniform. He stopped crying and started to pray God to bring his father home, if only for a day.

He didn't even see me standing by his side.

He kept on praying fervently.

I was happy, surrounded by my family, and that scene was strange to me.

Why so much suffering when his dad had died years ago?

His mother had never thought of starting over. Even Grandmother told her that if she remarried, her life would be better.

I learned that many kids had lost their dads because they had been murdered on duty in the street.

I didn't like to hear it, and I was sure it only happened to others.

But in our city, there were many crimes and troubles daily, and the thought that it could happen to my dad was sometimes getting into my head, but I quickly said to myself, "Not in my family!"

Every day I used to hear about troubles and tragedies all around me.

Innocent people, young people who were just starting their lives fell victims in the street.

Pain kept crawling into our city, and nobody could stop it.

There were times when Dad went to the funeral of his colleagues killed on duty.

When he came back home, he was very sad, and he used to lock himself in his room for hours.

Mom did her best to soothe him and stood by his side.

We the children were careful when we played our games and tried to make as little noise as possible.

But time was running wild, and things were slowly, slowly going their way.

Nobody came up with a solution to stop the tragedies.

There were way too many young people who were not interested in work. They wanted to make money fast, lots of money, and they didn't care about anything.

Drugs, fights between gangs, and thirst for sex made them live in a pathetic and permanent confusion.

The police were always called in, and many terrible situations were solved, but only for a short time.

They were looking for solutions, but the law continued to be broken. That was the only real problem.

The law was continuously ignored, and some people didn't even care.

Dad came to me and told me to get ready because Bill was joining us to go to the park.

In the park, we ran, played, and enjoyed a truly beautiful day.

Bill was always by my dad's side. He was talking and telling him stuff and asking him questions, and I didn't get the time to spend with my dad.

Mom was playing and running with George. She looked happy, and from time to time she would go to Dad to ask him something or give him a kiss.

Bill came near me and talked real fast. "I know you love your dad. He is so good to me and makes me feel good and strong like him. He's always teaching me good things, but you know he's not my like dad. I respect him a lot, and I want to see him, but the pain of losing your dad is too much, and this wound will never heal.

"I don't have a brother, and my loneliness is harder now. Mom is good, but she has lost the will power to be herself. She suffers quietly and doesn't know what to expect. I want to help her, and I am very proud when she asks me to do something for her, but that is very rare.

"Everything has changed. It feels like the world ended for us. For me and my mom. I'm always looking for something to bring me peace but can't find it. I'm an adult now, and I know that nobody can change my past. Once disaster strikes you, it fills your mind with bitterness and takes all your hopes away. But I have to keep on living somehow, and your dad helps me a lot. I need him, and please don't be mad if he spends so much time with me."

I was impressed that another boy, Bill, liked my dad so much.

I saw Bill as a brother, and what he said made feel good.

He needed my father, and my father made him feel good in his company, made him forget for a while the sadness and great tragedy that had fallen over their family.

How is it that so many and endless sufferings can be brought so fast on good people by young men who don't care about anything?

Killing to hide their deeds and doing unjustifiable things, they compromise themselves and bring a lot of misfortune on their own heads.

Many years in prison and no chance of rehabilitation.

Society tries to help you become a good, active member working for the welfare of society, but your lack of interest and your contempt for honest work, as well as your pursuit of money at all costs, push you to the fringe of society, and it is very hard to regain your balance.

When they release you from the penitentiary, you're like an animal.

Hardened by so much suffering and lack of love, discontent with what you've achieved as a human being in a free society, it is very difficult start a new, clean life, and most go back to prison.

For murders committed with extreme cruelty, they put you on death row, and your execution will take long years of tormented waiting, despair, fright, horror!

Nobody can explain it, and even worse, nobody seems to be able to find a solution.

The school tries to build your character, but if you obstinately refuse to participate in this long and sustained process, you place yourself outside the process and automatically deny yourself to be part of mainstream society.

There are many people involved in this education process and many children who are brought back to the right path.

Not all, though!

What a pity!

Some kids follow others and think they are smart and can they do what they want.

They don't care about anything.

Maybe those are the ones who should be forced to stay in school, but the law doesn't stipulate this obligation.

Social coexistence and respect for everyone is more important than the force of coercion. Nobody should be pressed or punished for lack of interest in school.

And these are the consequences!

The family is sometimes not interested, and the children have no supervision, or the parents left and abandoned them and don't care about them.

Forced to live with their grandparents or only one parent, children don't grow in healthy environment, in a climate of respect and responsibility.

As a result, they create they own false world that they follow against all common sense.

They're tough and they're strong.

Everybody should listen to them.

Nobody dare teach them anything because they know everything anyway.

My dad told me about some young people who, instead of going to school and study, prefer to hang around in the street and join gangs and start stealing stuff, selling drugs, raping, and attacking police with firearms.

On many occasions, my dad asked them why they were doing it.

Their answers were vague and didn't make any sense.

They didn't have any explanation, just the desire to do want they wanted.

The police knew them well and tried to take get out of that evil influence of that, without success.

They were convinced and determined to follow that path at all costs.

I know I'm a clear victim of those young people who shot my dad and then slashed him with their knives beyond recognition.

There were three young guys, and they admitted their crime in the court and showed no fear.

They said that was what's coming to all cops who would try to stand against them.

My hard life without a father and with a mom so harshly hit by fate has changed forever.

That is clear.

If it hadn't been my dad, it would have been another policeman who had to die serving society.

The police work is really a fight with death.

And the constant art of survival!

Many young guys have the wish to take revenge on a cop in their veins.

Therefore, when becoming a cop, you have to know from the start what lurks in the shadows for you.

A lawless society is impossible to conceive, and the policeman must be present among the people.

I keep tormenting myself with questions trying to understand why Dad became a policeman when there are so many other jobs out there.

We would be a happy family now, with no tragedies and endless pain.

I remember how wonderful were the days when Dad's colleagues used to come over and encourage us and offer support.

They were talking nicely about Dad and made me think that Dad hadn't died in vain and the respect for his sacrifice would serve as a model in people's lives.

# CHAPTER 3

# DICK NOW

"If he doesn't bring in something to eat, I'll throw him out of the house. I'm sick and tired of him. Now I am the master of this house," Dick said, looking at the empty fridge.

When Grandma died two years ago, I had to go on living with Grandpa, who did not know too much.

I had to help him with everything.

Anyway, it is better now.

Grandma insisted I should go to school every day and sometimes even do my homework.

Grandma was very strict and used to tell me, "Without education, your life is going to be hard, very hard."

The saddest day of my life was when Mom told me straightforward, "You're gonna live with your grandparents, and you're gonna be okay. My new boyfriend has three children, and there is no more room for you in the house. Your dad is away, he should help you, and besides, I don't even know where he is!"

I cried and cried the whole day.

Humph, right on my fourteenth birthday.

Life with the grandparents was so-and-so. But what could I do, I had to live somewhere.

My friends the same as me helped me.

The first drugs I took made feel strong.

Soon, I gave up school, and the chicks in our black community loved me.

They were good and passionate when they touched my boner.

My grandpa was easy to lie to.

"How're you doing?"

"School is good. Pretty soon I'm gonna graduate and go on to high school. Don't you worry, I know what I gotta do now!"

Mom had completely forgotten about me.

The next two birthdays I had, she didn't come to see me.

I wanted to go and see her, but I had no idea where she lived.

She had never let me know what her new address was. I guess she lived in another state.

Which one? Who knows?

Because I was coming home very late at night every night, Grandpa told me to leave his house. That's when I told him to his face, "If you keep talking like this, I'm gonna throw you out of the house. Therefore, keep your mouth shut."

Larry, a guy in the same situation as me, asked me to keep his gun for a few days.

He said he was gonna tell me why.

It was easy 'cause Grandpa couldn't see or hear too well.

I could do whatever I wanted.

The drugs I did with my friends gave me moments of ecstasy, and the days went on all the same.

The chicks were riding my dick and were crazy to mount it.

The house belonged to my grandpa, and he was still paying some debts.

He had fought in a war, I don't know which one, but I know he received a very small sum of money every third Wednesday of the month.

Good for him.

I was trying to make ends meet with some stuff I found in the neighborhood and fend for myself.

One day, Larry came to me, and he was in a hurry. He said we had a good opportunity how to make some fast cash.

Around seven that evening, Reik would order a pizza delivered to his house, and when that poor bastard would come to deliver the hot pizza, we would follow him and steal all his cash.

Reik lived on the tenth floor in a building on Main Street.

We went there and saw the guy delivering the pizza.

We blocked the two elevators and waited for Reik's signal.

It was short: "He's gone."

We split in two groups, one group on a set of stairs, another group on the other. The building had two entrances and two elevators.

We waited for the guy to call the elevators, but they were blocked.

Nobody noticed because in the building, the elevators were always out of order.

We climbed the stairs.

My heart was beating faster and faster.

The pizza guy was waiting for the elevator on the tenth floor.

Real fast, a couple of seconds, Larry pulled up a knife and slashed his face, ears, and nose and asked for the money.

The guy was about our age. He understood he couldn't run away and stayed calm when I got my hand into his pocket and took his papers and his money.

All of it!

After I took all the money from his wallet, I dumped it in the street. I was scared.

We split the cash equally, and then we ran away.

Twenty minutes later, I got worried, and I went back to the building to take the wallet because the police might find my fingerprints on it.

There was a cop car in front of the building. I got scared, and I gave up.

I knew when my grandpa received his payments, and I always stole half of it.

Anyway, I don't think he realized anything. He was always sleepy and couldn't see or hear well.

Once, I took almost all the money. I needed to pay Martin for the new drugs.

That guy counted every penny. You couldn't get anything past him.

One day, when I had no cash, he refused to give me any drugs, not even to sniff it.

That was why I stole one of his little bags.

He saw me and jump on me like a tiger.

"I'll gonna kill you right now. Give it back. I'm gonna really kill you 'cause they gonna kill me if I don't give all the money in time."

In this business, you had to play straight. Otherwise, you lose everything.

No one had any mercy and time for talk. Everything was about the dough.

Last month, they shot and killed Lee because he was four days late to pay up.

Just like that. *Bang, bang!*

I'm not lying. I was there and saw it.

I wanted to run away, but they said, "Don't think you can just hide. We know everything."

When Grandpa realized some of his money was missing, he came to me and asked me.

I pretended I was so mad that Grandpa got scared and left and didn't say anything.

You gotta be a fast talker if you don't wanna starve.

What else could I do?

I felt pity for Grandpa, but what was I supposed to do?

Ever since, Grandpa started hiding his money in another place, but it took me no time to find it.

One day, Grandpa asked to go and buy something from the pharmacy because he had great pains in his belly.

I went there and paid three bucks for some pills.

I didn't give him back the change. What the fuck, I gotta eat too!

Grandpa didn't ask for the change. I guess he forgot about it.

He was lying in bed, and I could see the pain on his face.

I helped him take one pill, and he seemed to feel better.

I wasn't sure, but it looked like that.

I went out to meet Larry. He was my best friend.

He didn't refuse anything I asked him.

He had some coins, and we decided to go get something at McDonald's.

His life was a carbon copy of mine.

He did what he wanted and didn't listen to anyone, unless he was afraid.

# CHAPTER 4

# MR. JACK

One day, I had a friendly encounter with Mr. Jack, a black guy in our community who used to say all the time, "You help me, I'll help you."

Together with other guys my age, I broke into six homes belonging to white people and two restaurants.

The money we got was good for buying dope little gifts for the chicks, and something to eat.

Today, as usual, I went to the park to meet Larry.

I'd waited for about three hours, but he didn't show up.

It seemed strange, and just when I was about to quit, a familiar voice called my name.

It was Mr. Jack.

He invited me to get a bite at McDonald's.

Ten minutes later, Mr. Jack nervously told me that Larry killed a chick from the hood and her boyfriend.

When the cops came, Larry refused to surrender and shot a cop in the left eye.

He was taken to the police precinct, and the wounded cop who had a little chance to survive was taken to the emergency.

I was really scared, but Mr. Jack told me to relax because our black community was well protected by the government and that the president, the Department of Justice chief, and some other important black leaders were working on that full-time.

Everything was gonna be fine.

Mr. Jack told me stuff I had never heard before, not even in school.

"You gotta know that blacks were slaves in America. These white animals invaded our land in Africa, chased us, and put us in chains, forcefully brought us here, away from our wonderful land, where we used to have everything. These white animals forced us to change our names, eat, and do whatever they liked.

"Read Kunta Kinte's story, and you'll become a real black. The whites, all of them, gotta pay for everything. Nothing is too much for the trouble they made for our families in Africa. And for what? To harvest their cotton for them?

"It's true that most slave owners were nice people, took care of their slaves when they were sick, gave them food, baptized their children born in their household. But even if only one white guy was mean, all whites must pay up for this. There won't be any peace until then."

"Now they gotta give us their houses, their white wives and daughters, their jobs, absolutely everything! The white people, men and women, must pay up. Our hatred of the white people shall never disappear. Quite the opposite, we must make sure our hate doesn't disappear and make any white suffer.

"You know, there are blacks now who hold high social positions, have great power. Well, those black are more determined than ever to destroy the white people, to humiliate them, and to help other black to dominate in all the fields. You've seen black communities starting riots in the street. What do you think? You think they do this on their own? No sirree, bub! They are encouraged, indoctrinated, paid, and pushed to destroy the whites and their businesses as hard as they can. Millions of dollars, maybe even billions, are invested in this secret war against the whites.

"We will win for sure, we got our people, agitators paid to keep the flame of hate going. The big guys take care of us. They don't want peace! Al Sharpton has precise instructions and tasks. I told you, we're well organized, see? The big guys want the war, but in secret and out of sight. The end justifies the means, just like the president or some important guy said.

"The whites must be killed slowly but surely. We're lucky the white don't have the slightest idea what we're planning against them. Not far from here, in Baltimore, the blacks already started the war against police. Isn't it funny how the blacks threw sticks and stones at the cops while the cops had been ordered by our black chiefs in power to let the blacks riot and even make room for them to loot the stores. Everything was done according to a plan.

"We are strong. The white are trying to defend themselves, but they are confused. We must slowly and patiently destroy the police force so that nobody is protected anymore. That day is not far away. All the whites will be destroyed, humiliated, eliminated, and we the blacks will take everything away from them for free.

"Isn't it great? What do you think? All the whites will be thrown out of their houses, and we will immediately take their place. The ones who will oppose us, if any, will be shot on the spot. It's not too difficult because millions of white women are married to black guys and are totally under their control.

"Can't you see that the people in power started to mock the concept of police? The total war against police has started. The idea that police is stupid, police is racist. 'What we want? Death to police! When? Right now! "All of these things are in preparation of the final assault. Victory is in the air! Soon, very soon, the whites will be terminated.

"We blacks don't sit idle. We're always inventing something, inventing to keep the whites under pressure. The Fergusson slogan 'Don't stop us! Don't shoot!' has been unfortunately compromised and proved to be a big lie. But it's okay. We don't sit idle. We're always inventing something. Inventing to keep the whites under pressure. The recent Black Lives Matter has proved to be great success, and we'll keep moving forward."

I don't really get it, but it seems to work.

---

We've got some problems with some of our black brothers who don't understand reality and want to denounce our leaders who hold important positions in the state.

These peaceful blacks have understood the situation and would like to make the other blacks realize the danger they are facing.

We must not let them do it.

There must never be peace.

How could Al Sharpton and other black people in high positions spend millions of dollars, live a great life, and enjoy total power if there was peace?

Our people high up told us clearly that the whites will destroy everything we have accomplished so far.

We must support them to keep them in power.

And they will help us.

No, there'll never be peace because our black leaders in high positions will make sure of that.

Those idiots have started to speak out loud even on TV. And there is more and more of them.

They don't want to accept it under any circumstance.

Some of them are our priests, and people believe them.

But I'm pretty sure that the higher-ups will tone them down, I have no doubts about it.

They are like a storm in a teacup.

The great black masses follow us all the way. We have well-paid agitators working for us.

It's their job now. They have free rein from the bosses.

We got a few small problems, but there are so many people believing in our bosses that they just don't give a shit.

---

I was speechless.

So that was it, the whites force us from our beloved Africa to come to America to be their slaves?

They changed our lives, our names, and our traditions and beat us humiliates us and put us to work around the clock? Now I understand why the blacks hate the whites so much!

I went back home. I was furious.

All right then, the whites are guilty must pay for it.

No justice, no peace.

Now I understand why blacks rioted against the police and the whites.

Why so many killings on both sides, black and white?

That's how the entire population of America is separated in to opposing camps.

Blacks and whites, yeah!

Mr. Jack opened up my mind.

What a fool I used to be.

# CHAPTER 5

# MY GOOD, BELOVED FATHER

The phone rang suddenly.

Even the phone ring had a different feel.

I lunged to grab the phone, but I was so agitated and scared that I dropped it and the phone went dead.

No chance to talk to somebody.

I saw a black car stopping in front of the house. I was surprised. It was not my dad's car.

My mom came out with the help of a gentleman.

She was sobbing and crying her heart out. George started crying too, without really understanding what was going on.

My first thought was, *Something bad has happened to my father. Oh no, God! Not my dad! Please, God! No! Not my dear dad! God, please be good to us! Better take me, not my dad, right now, please! God, take me now! I won't be able to live without my dad!*

There is an icon of God in my bedroom, and in desperation, I knelt before it and started to implore God to take care of my dad and not take him from us.

Tears were rolling on my cheeks, and I didn't know what to do.

It was clear now.

My dad had been wounded and might be in a serious condition in the hospital.

"Which hospital? I'll run there and kneel in front of the doctors and beg them not to let him die. I need him too much. Maybe the doctors will understand and will save my dad. Oh, God, please take pity to us! God, please let us get back to our life before. God, I think you can make a miracle and save my dad. Without my dad, I'll be nothing."

I felt a warm hand on my shoulder, and I understood. It was mom, and she was drained.

She tried to soothe me, but she collapsed on the floor. She was unconscious.

At this point, I was truly desperate.

"What should I do now? God, please don't take my mom, too! God, help us, don't leave us desperate here! What did we do wrong? How did we sin before you? How can such a happy family become so miserable all of a sudden?"

It was too much for a child's heart.

The gentleman who drove Mom home called on his cell phone, and we waited for someone to come over and help Mom.

George had fallen asleep on the sofa, and nobody was taking care of him.

He was so young, and his life had changed so dramatically.

And mine, too.

Like a hurricane, heavy misfortunes descended on our home that used to be so happy.

Things happened just like that. There was no easy answer.

Why?

Everything was so confusing, baffling, and unexpected.

There is a God, and Mom always told us to pray to him because he will help us in life.

I'd always prayed, and I'd never asked too much. I just asked to have Mom and Dad and George by my side at all times.

I'd never asked for anything but health for my family.

I knew that being a policeman, Dad's job was a hard and dangerous one.

I'd never understood why he was doing it, but he had been doing this job all his life.

I was sure he could handle any situation and that nothing could make him fall down.

I had no premonition or feeling that Dad could leave us without saying his last words to us.

There was too much grief in this world, and we were so helpless!

I was preparing to go to high school.

I can't remember if Dad gave me advice what to become in my life.

He was sure there was enough time for that.

It wasn't so. He had no time at all.

He disappeared like a shooting star and left us and went far away from us forever.

I didn't know what to do all by myself. He didn't even give me a single piece of advice that I could follow.

What I should learn in life to avoid evil deeds? How I should help Mom or George?

If the world only knew how unfair it is to lose your daddy and never be able to see him, ask for his advice, get his help when you need to be protected from evil things, and make you enjoy your life as a child.

From now on, we'd only have Mom with us, and the thought that she might die too simply horrified me.

Mom must defend us and care for us now.

How could poor Mom, destroyed by Dad's tragic death, defend us?

She was the one who needed help first!

She was alone with two small children.

She was so desperate after Dad's death that who knows if she'd ever recover.

She was just a poor, sad, tormented mom.

Her weeping was breaking my heart, and she was praying God for mercy.

She still couldn't believe that it was true and hoped for a miracle!

Mom was the most traumatized by Dad's death.

I understood that Mom needed our help more than we needed hers.

God would know how many misfortunes would come over us.

For a moment, I became more alert and apprehensive.

Mom needed a lot of help.

Maybe more than us, her good and loving kids.

I was thinking if our grandparents lived, they could have come and stayed with us. I don't know how, but all our grandparents were not alive anymore.

When they talked about them, Mom and Dad said something about a plane crash and also about a car driven by some stoned white people who sped and smashed them and killed them on the spot.

I'd often thought about how nice it was to have grandparents, but I couldn't remember much about them.

Scott too didn't have grandparents and was always sorry about that.

For Easter or Christmas, we used to be invited to Dad's friends.

There were a lot of people and joy and so much cake that George couldn't have enough of it.

I was absolutely delighted. I was happy.

Mom and Dad together with us kids.

But I remember what Mom said once, "Dan, George, come over here to talk to Darwen's grandparents."

Darwen was a boy the same age as me, and he couldn't walk.

He was sitting in a wheelchair all the time.

His grandparents were so young I thought they were his parents.

His grandparents talked to us very nicely, and Mom was very proud she had so handsome and healthy kids.

I felt it.

I found out why Darwen was alone with his grandparents and crippled.

He couldn't walk at all.

One day when he was with his family driving to farm, a huge truck smashed at high speed into their car, a Volkswagen Beetle.

His parents died on the way to the hospital.

Two months later, the doctors at the hospital said they did the best they could for him after that terrible accident. They save his life, but not his crushed legs.

But all these were just memories now.

Now I had in front of me a mother who must accept the unfair death of the father of her children.

I abruptly returned to the cruel inescapable reality.

Yes, before me was my father, who had died on duty.

# CHAPTER 6

# DICK'S PREDICAMENT

For a few days, I didn't get out of the house.

I was very scared and thought that the blacks' riot against the whites was going to begin soon.

Everything was very clear in Mr. Jack's mind.

I had a headache.

What was I to understand?

Mr. Jack presented in a documented and persuasive way a terrible situation in the near future.

I didn't really get the meaning of things, nor how things would evolve after the assured victory of the blacks against the white beasts.

I went to the fridge to grab something, but it was empty. That was why I went out to the corner store to buy something to eat and drink a Pepsi.

Grandfather was in the bed, and I don't think he had gotten out of bed recently.

Before I went out, I grabbed some change from his wallet.

Maybe he needed something too, but I was too agitated and excited to care about him.

I was not in the mood for anything really.

It was quiet in the street.

All of a sudden, Tom came up to me.

# THE DEATH PENALTY FOR KARL MARX

Tom was some kind of relative of my grandfather.

I tried to avoid him and pretend I hadn't seen him.

"How're you do in', boy? How's Grandpop? Is he all right? If I got some time tomorrow, I'll come see him."

Then he took a long look at me and said, "Is it just my impression, or is you in a bad mood? Come with me to Thil's house to repair something for him, and then we'll go grab a bite."

I'd never liked to talk to Tom, but I was so troubled and confused that I didn't refuse him as usual.

The repair at Thil's place didn't take too long, I don't even know how long.

In my mind I saw blacks attacking whites and whites attacking blacks.

It was all bad.

What the heck, I saw war.

Tom was stout and known to be a good fighter. Nobody in our black community could take him.

His strong fists could smash anything. I felt small and ridicule beside him, but we went to restaurant to eat something.

I was starving, really.

It just happened that the staff was composed of blacks and white who served us very friendly with everything we ordered.

I was shocked.

Only a few days ago, Mr. Jack had told me about the white criminals and the blacks' war against them and about their certain and right death.

Tom was watching me and said, "What's bothering you? Speak out and stop tormenting yourself. Whom did you kill? See what we can do."

I was puzzled how Tom guessed my mood. I decided to tell him everything I had learned recently.

"Tom, you know Mr. Jack, don't you?"

"Yeah," said Tom. "And so what?"

Like a machine gun, I spat out everything Mr. Jack had told me.

Tom stared at me and said with a faint smile on his face, "Let's take it easy, boy. Blacks don't like whites, yeah! Why? Because the whites forcefully brought blacks to America to be their slaves. I've never liked this dirty job. But that was a long, long time ago. It's true, some suffered more or less. But it was too long ago to care now. Long time ago. That was then.

"Revenge is useless. And we should take revenge on whom? On some people who weren't even born at that time and didn't benefit in any way from it! A lot of blacks want revenge today saying it's moral and fair to get reparation. But who?

"Some smart blacks were fast in seeing a good opportunity to make some money. It's true, some have made and are still making good money on that. There are others who joined several black militant organizations with the clear goal to get revenge at any cost! They created pompously named societies, allegedly for betterment of the blacks, that in reality are just a means to make good money for themselves.

"The National Action Group or the Black Panthers Party and many others like that have been working with a clear purpose of poisoning the atmosphere, to make sure there will never be peace, and to fool and buy the blacks in order to start riotingin the streets and demanding rights all the time. It's a permanent nondescript army ready to execute any order without asking questions.

"Do you think this is good? To keep them under total control and obedient, from time to time they throw them some reasons for hate which at first confrontation with reality prove to be detrimental to themselves. But the big bosses crave power, and the black masses don't have time to ask if it's good or bad.

"Can they offer them any jobs, housing or money, and a quiet life? They'll just enroll them on the dole lists, also called Social Assistance, and it's enough for them. Our higher-up bosses are very smart! They know that only if you fool the masses, you can control them.

"*Justice* is just an empty word. Blacks will never have what they want. Only some of them. The others must serve. But whites are not doing any better. You know how many whites are homeless and begging in the street? That's right. Years ago you could see armies of homeless blacks begging in the street. Now armies of whites have replaced them with patriotic pride. Blacks are up.

"Nevertheless, blacks will have to wait. The trick is to throw them a couple of bucks from time to time to keep them from starving to death and to keep the flame of hate against the whites burning and always present as a justification for the incompetence of our leaders. The blacks will do as they're told.

"But our leaders know that hate is not enough and turn any unintended event between police and blacks into a deliberate act against all blacks. How about the law? How about logic? No explanation or evidence that those who broke the law were wrong. Nooo! There is no such thing in the black community.

"It's demonstrated, blacks can't be wrong. They say that blacks are deliberately targeted, hunted down, and killed for no reason. Just because they are black. Is that so? Is it true or not? It doesn't matter. That works for them, so it's all good. No explanation whether they killed for a reason or not, why they refused to put their gun down and give up, that they shoot at any cop with no mercy, that they rape black and white girls as they wish, they break into homes and kill the owners, of course, after fucking their wives or daughters of even sons in that home. What law? They are black and whites have to pay. They must always pay."

In a shy voice, I said, "But I've seen whites doing the same things, so––"

"Yes," said Tom, "whites do the same, and they go to jail for their crimes. They deserve it. Justice must be served in their case. They're whites, like I said. But for blacks, it's something else, very different. Blacks were brought here to be slaves! Therefore, now they get their revenge against the whites and the whites can't do anything about it.

"We blacks people have more rights today than ever. Why? Do you think it's a gift? Forget it. Everything is planned. Our leaders don't sleep at night. They monitor and make sure that we keep pressure on the whites at all times, scare them, stress them, push them to do what we want them to do. They got another trouble on their heads now. To be labeled a racist is a big personal problem. See how smart our bosses are? Simple and efficient.

"If you're a white, you lose, you can lose everything. Your money, your job, your company, your family, social status, and pretty soon your freedom. You can be put in jail for a long time or forever! Who cares? You think it's a joke to be labeled a racist? See?

"Our bosses are relentlessly coming up with something new to get closer to the day of victory when the whites are terminated. God help us! And the stupid whites are playing right into their hands every time. They didn't understand the danger. Quite the opposite, they're helping for their own demise.

"That's how, slowly but surely, we're riding them, and they don't dare say anything. Our leaders are more powerful than ever, and justice is in their hands too. They are under control, and the justice people are afraid of our bosses."

Tom startled me when he stood up suddenly and said, "All TV channels are talking about this situation day and night. Journalists, politicians, editors, radio commentators present the situation just like I explained it to you. Okay, enough talk. Don't forget, I'll drop by tomorrow to see your grandpop."

He paid for the meals and then said out loud, "See you tomorrow," and disappeared fast.

# CHAPTER 7

# GARY EXPLAINED IT WELL

Sometime later, I met this guy who used to be a journalist.

He was tall, handsome, young black guy that all the girls wanted.

His name was Gary.

When he saw me, he said, "Hey, Dick! How are you? Are you doing well?"

He just said that because he didn't really care about anybody.

I knew quite well.

I remember one day, Gary saw me in the street, and for the next two days, I worked to clean up his backyard for ten bucks.

After I finished everything he asked me to do, he gave me five more bucks.

---

He always had a white girlfriend.

He would sometimes invite them in his house for dinner.

His father had died a long time ago.

Some problems with his prostate. I had no idea what that was.

But he died young.

All I know was that he was smart and talked a lot.

He knew everything.

First, politics.

You didn't even need to ask him anything, and he would start talking and kept talking for hours.

We sat down in the shade in front of a café.

We started talking about the hood.

He said everyone in the hood must do as told by Mr. Jack and a few others. He said he hadn't seen cops around for some time, just more ambulances than before.

I was still scared about what Mr. Jack and Tom had told me.

I asked him what he thought about the blacks' war against the whites. And about the big boss high up there who always defended us.

He was just waiting for a question. He started talking without any interruptions.

"One day, OBAMA publicly declared that whatever he does, the Republicans oppose it because he is black. Right away, people came up to his defense. This guy, Holder, Eric Holder, OBAMA's friend, he's just a smart guy."

He pondered for a while.

"How could they stop and control the slightest opposition to OBAMA? He told them that some white are opposed to Hussein OBAMA because he's black, and all the whites shitted their pants. They all fell down!

"Of course, it was not true. Basically, who cares if he's black. His master, OBAMA, does all kinds of stupid, shitty things and undoubtedly demonstrates with leftist revolutionary enthusiasm every day that he was totally unqualified for such a big responsibility. Well! It doesn't matter at all. The important thing is that they stay in power. America may as well crumble! Ever since then, the racist label has been working like a charm. It's cyanide, it kills everything."

I tentatively asked him, "How did OBAMA get to the White House?"

# THE DEATH PENALTY FOR KARL MARX

"What the hell are you talking about, boy?"

He looked at his watch and said, "Okay, I still got some time," and started to talk again like a machine gun.

I was all ears. I might not be as smart as he was, but I understood fast where he was leading.

He went at it again. "I may be black, but I get politics very well. That fact that OBAMA is totally unfit for the White House, that he's got almost no experience, that he has been on welfare all his life, all that doesn't matter. In order to polish him a bit, they gave him the highly scientific and honorary title of Community Organizer. Who the hell ever heard of this before? There is no such profession.

"See? Blacks are inventive. The ones at the very top. Don't get excited. These Liberals are a party composed mainly of modest people with a lot of personal problems. Look at poor Nancy. She can hardly stand up and make a speech, and her head is trembling all the time you'd think she's gonna kick the bucket. How about Harry, the Senate chief? The big kahuna! Big crook. Devious and shifty as a chameleon. If he says something today, you can bet tomorrow he'll say the opposite. He's in a political competition with John, the guy who's lying through his teeth all the time."

I asked, "Which John?"

"What do you mean which John? John Kerry! The ugly guy with the long face you do not know where it finishes. More recently he got himself a pair of brand-new crutches. Yeah! But real high-tech crutches, special order from Austria. What do you think?

"So how's the Liberal Party doing? The old Ted Kennedy has tried all the tricks in the book. Nothing. But with an enlightened mind and a clutched hand, he has found it.

"How could they win sweet as honey power? How could they win the elections? He's studied the history of presidential elections and found out in great awe and revolutionary enthusiasm the solution.

A super simple one. Much too simple. Wonder how those stupid Republicans never thought about it. Our good luck. Hooray! Hooray!

"In their pitiful minds, they understood that their political end was near and decided to hang on to poor OBAMA to get them out the shithole. And the burden was dumped on him. Finally OBAMA understood what the game was and liked the idea very much. Can you imagine, getting such a gift out of the blue? You gotta be a fool to refuse it. That's good.

"As I was telling you, Uncle Ted learned with stupefaction that the blacks could never be bothered to vote for white people. The voting thing had nothing to do with them. Let the whites worry about that. In his wise mind, a light shone up and understood what needed to be done. Blacks must be used again. The must all be made to come to vote, not like before when a meager percentage participated.

"Enough with this fear of losing power. The glimmer of hope for victory filled the Liberals' darkened hearts. Sir Kennedy then said in strong and loud voice, 'Be it Barak OBAMA, or OBAMA Barak, it's the same thing.' Yeah!

"In fact, he had never heard about that guy. He had been a senator for some time, but he didn't stand out with anything. It doesn't matter as long as it does the job. That will get the blacks out their homes and come to vote. Just think of the political slogans of the election year, 'A Black in the White House' or 'First Black American President.'

"Sure thing, it's gonna be the greatest sting for the Republicans, their personal enemies. Hooray! Hooray! The Liberal Party in power again pretty soon and maybe forever if we're smart about it. SomeLiberal had some reservations. If you think about it, why not? It was worth the risk. Actually, there was no risk. There was nothing better anyway. That's a good one. Hillary was too soft to win. In politics, you gotta be fast-thinking and glib. Otherwise, your sting will fail."

Let me get back to the whites' trouble with racism.

You see that blacks don't just sit idle. They're always inventing something.

And the whites are frightened not be called racist because all hell will fall on their heads.

Many lost their money, homes, rights, and job.

If the masquerade doesn't stop, pretty soon all those labeled racist may go to jail for a long time or forever.

Who gives a shit about them?

Pretty soon they'll regret ever being born white. Ha, ha, ha!

There must one honest person to stop this black terror against innocent people.

*Politically correct* is very bad.

Honestly, nobody wants to kill blacks or take away their rights or something like that.

The whites are minding their business and accept anything from us.

I was really surprised to learn that a few days ago a very young white guy killed several blacks in one of their churches.

That's not good at all.

Any murder is abominable and should be stopped somehow.

He justified his crime in a most strange manner. He said, "You blacks rape and take all of our white girls and have got too much power over the whites."

It drives you nuts when you see the way OBAMA lies and stirs the black community.

As soon as you criticize or tell the truth as it is, they hit you with *racism* in the head.

Too much terror against the whites and, I swear, for no reason.

Yesterday I was talking to a good friend of mine who is white. We went to college together.

A well-mannered and respectful guy. You wouldn't hear this guy saying a dirty word.

Really, too nice for his age.

And too weak.

He told me something that blew my mind.

Now blacks got smarter.

Brother, they'll do anything, say anything, and demand anything.

Life's sweet, what can I say.

But none of the whites has ever had the guts to tell this truth.

My friend from Queens told me something terrible, because he's white and therefore always the blacks' target.

The man was going down the stairs from his floor.

In front of the elevator, there were several people and two blacks with travel suitcases. The man was in a hurry, and he walked carefully and respectfully between the wall and the black who was standing in front of the elevator.

After he came out of the building, a female voice started yelling so loud you'd think somebody was trying to kill her. She was yelling real loud!

"Listen! Listen! Hold on. Stop. Hey, listen!"

He didn't even need to stop because she was running toward him like a horse.

She was short and sweating all over, and she lunged at him and shouted in a booming voice, "How dare you push my dad? Because he's black, eh? Because he's black, eh? Some people told me they saw you doing it."

She was right in front of the elevator with her father. Why did she need to ask others?

She clearly saw that I didn't push or touch anyone. Anyway, there was plenty of room for a skinny guy like me to walk between the wall and the black guy.

She shouted at me, "You're a racist, you racist! Racist! Racist! Racist! Racist! Racist! Racist!"

She wouldn't stop shouting.

I was on the sidewalk in front of the building and a lot people.

I said, "I apologize, but I swear to God I didn't do that. I am very careful and respectful with everyone. If I touched him, please accept my apologies."

She yelled "Racist!" again, and then with a smile on her face, she left.

---

Of course, this has nothing to do with racism. Even if by mistake you pushed him a bit when you walked by him, that was not racism.

I didn't touch him at all. She knew that very well.

But who cares about the truth?

She didn't need any truth!

He was white and needed to be terrorized and frightened and eventually punished!

But in her face, in the posture of her body, in her tone of voice, I saw so much hatred, hostility, passion, rage, fury, desire to humiliate me at any price, to use the *racist* word, that was truly horrifying.

She was sweating out of delight.

Now she was another black woman.

She was no longer sweating. Now she was calm and had good reasons to be proud!

She had taught a white man what his place was.

She made a white guy be afraid of her.

She had started and couldn't stop.

I think she would have shot me on the spot, mercilessly and without blinking.

For her I was a white guy who needed to be taught a lesson, to make me understand that now blacks are in power and that we must start to respect them as royalty.

No matter what.

No more dicking around with them.

---

Several neighbors who were having a chat in front of the entrance hall and who knew me well were totally surprised and told me grudgingly, "Oh my god, what a world we live in with OBAMA's racism! There's something rotten in America!"

"Yeah."

"It's no good being a racist, and you shouldn't be."

But now because of OBAMA, who desperately clings to power, he stirred all black with something that doesn't exist.

I understood very clearly.

Racism, even imaginary, expresses perfectly the blacks' discontent of being different from the whites and because they know they will always be like that.

It is the expression of the incapacity of keeping the whites under their domination showing total respect.

They know they got lots of troubles, and the culprits must always be the whites.

The Liberals should publish a book about racism so that everyone knows what's allowed and what's not allowed to avoid being called a racist.

People need an antiracism guide in order to avoid making mistakes!

A black retired guy I know and have a chat every day told me, "Don't be afraid. They are completely blinded by OBAMA. It's a very dangerous idea for them too. It's ideological. It'll creep down into your soul, and then all revenge against a white guy, guilty or innocent, constitutes a great relief. And so on. Long live racism. It's a shame."

America is fast approaching big troubles.

I have sometimes wondered, "How can you totally dominate whites?"

They are more numerous than us and many more. Millions are coming all the time.

Chinese, Latinos, Europeans.

There is no way for us to surpass them in numbers.

I think that OBAMA should stop his hatred of whites, who, honestly speaking, are all right.

That is why a lot of whites start to dislike the blacks and change their opinion about them.

Pretty soon they will lose a lot.

Even the blacks.

See?

Even today, here many whites had such a bad impression of the wild black woman shouting racism, that they express it out loud.

"OBAMA is killing us all."

"Hate is not good at all."

It's true that the whites are not too happy living together with the blacks.

But it will always be like that.

Many blacks are very unhappy with the whites and even with the blacks in many instances.

But in today's world, any black can simply destroy a white guy by accusing him of racism!

Therefore, we cannot go on categorizing and punishing people for nothing.

Even Dr. Luther King was totally against violence, and he was betrayed and shot by a black man out of jealousy.

The story with the whites involved in his death is just a fairy tale.

Doesn't work with me!

"We know that he was fucking some black dude's wife and this guy was jealous and cut it off."

"What?"

"His life, what did you think?

Hey!

"I don't like to talk about this dirty friggin' story."

You see, I'm black, and honestly I voted for OBAMA the first and the second time.

And if OBAMA is a candidate again, I'll still vote for him.

A black president makes me feel good, stronger, and I feel I have more security.

This may be a false feeling, but that's it.

Many black people think like that.

If I have a black boss at work, I feel empowered.

If the boss is white, it's too much effort to exist.

We can't just brush aside these realities with words. Today's racism doesn't exist, but it's a thick concrete wall against the slightest chance that a black guy might lose anything.

The whites must understand that blacks are strong and tough.

Why do you think black people jump up instinctively when there is a riot? So as to avoid anything that might be against them.

White people don't think about it, but it's good to scare them and keep them on their toes, under total control. OBAMA is smart when it comes to that.

I told you all this so you understand that we know everything and we're ready for anything if OBAMA calls on us.

I only watch TV and listen to the radio or read some newspapers to learn about racism.

I left Gary a bit smarter and with some clear ideas in my head.

Would there be a better solution to work for both blacks and whites?

Or will the situation always be like that?

Gary said that blacks are united and nothing could divide them.

It's true that white are more selfish, don't defend themselves, and are not as united as we are.

# CHAPTER 8

## DICK AND HIS WORLD

When I got back home, Grandpa had fallen from the bed and was mumbling something I didn't understand. I raised him back to his bed and tried to help him.

I didn't know what to do.

It was the first time.

I gave him some water because I didn't have anything else.

I took his arm to tuck it under the bed sheet. Holy shit, his arm and hand were limp and cold like a dead man's.

I remember that Lachy Loreta used to come to him and stay until late.

She was kind of a community nurse. People said that she always used to steal something from your house when she left.

I wanted to call her, but I didn't have her phone number, not to mention her address.

Suddenly, I remembered that Tom was supposed to come and visit Grandpa.

But I had to help him somehow. I went out in the street to get help from neighbors.

Jarly was home.

She was sitting on three-legged chair in front of her house and swinging.

I asked her advice.

She told me to call the ambulance, and I did.

The dispatcher asked me his age, and I said, "Ninety."

Actually I had no idea. The guy said, "We'll be there as soon as possible."

Later, an ambulance showed up and took Grandpa to the hospital.

They didn't tell me which one.

I was happy to be all by myself in the house.

Absolutely on my own.

An idea struck me.

"What if Grandpa dies?"

Well, that wasn't too bad. But who was gonna pay the bills that were sure to keep coming?

Fuck it!

Too many troubles on my shoulders.

I gotta see Mr. Jack. He'd teach me what to do.

But where could I find him?

---

I remembered what Larry used to say.

"When in trouble, take some dope, and everything will be solved like a charm."

I pulled out my dope box from under the bed. It was well hidden to be hard to find.

Shit! Not too much left.

But I took one right away and waited.

Somebody knocked on the door and wanted togo and open it.

Fuck! I couldn't stand up.

It was too late. The dope had kicked in.

I was happy.

Around me everything was blue, pink, beautiful, full of many colors.

Amazing colors.

Wow! Now I felt like a new man.

Strong, happy, with dreams hard to describe or understand.

Something warm was oozing under me.

I think I pissed or shitted myself.

So what!

I was in paradise.

---

I felt a strong hand gripping my arm. Somebody was trying to lift me from the floor.

I started yelling at him, "No! No! Leave me alone! You asshole, what do you want from me now? Don't ruin my happiness. I'm in my own house and I feel so good. What the hell do you want? Let me be, it's my life."

I started to howl and kicked him and punched him. But I felt totally powerless. I had no control over my movements, and the horror of being paralyzed was choking me.

"What happened to me?" I asked myself in desperation.

Tyrone, a guy who had helped me break into a few houses, was near me and was desperately trying to tell me something.

"Mr. Jack sent me to get you. He wants to see you. He's got something special. Come to the park when you sober up."

And he left.

Mr. Jack?

Who the fuck was that?

And what did he want from me?

No! I didn't know him, and I wanna be left alone.

Slowly I started to wake up.

The fact that Mr. Jack wanted to see me came right on time.

That was exactly what I wanted! I needed badly to see him, to get his advice what to do and so many other things.

I stood up from the floor.

Fuck!

An excruciating pain shot through my head.

I was blinded for a moment.

A violent, deafening buzz was ringing in my ears.

My attempt to get up and go to the park to meet Mr. Jack failed rapidly.

I had no power at all, and a strong nausea sensation came over me. I couldn't even feel my legs.

I was helpless and terrified I was gonna stay like that.

I was lying on the floor, dirty with my own shit that stank to high heaven, and the world didn't make any sense to me.

Could it be from the dope?

But I'd taken dope many times, and it was never like that.

I think that Martin wanted to kill me.

Ma, wait till I see him!

I remember he asked five bucks for a bag of dope, but I gave him only three 'cause I didn't have more.

Now I remember. Yes! Yes! Yes! He switched the bag and said that was better for me.

Then he gave me a friendly advice, "Less money will buy you more. Why should you pay so much? You're a nice but poor boy."

So that was it.

He sold me cheaper dope.

But very bad dope, real bad!

I was gonna kill him when I'd see him! He'd see what was coming to him!

Later in the evening I gathered some strength.

Not much but a little better.

I was tired, tormented by fear, and afraid I was not going to be able to stand up.

I felt like I was beaten with baseball bat.

My arms and legs were in great pain, and I didn'tknow what to do.

I didn't know how to heal myself.

It was getting dark outside and a pale ray of light was shining in the darkened room.

A room stinking of piss and shit.

My mind hadn't cleared up, but I knew I hadto wash fast. Otherwise, I was going to die of stink for sure.

I washed in the bathroom but couldn't find any towel.

I didn't know what Grandpa was doing in this house.

I opened up a closet with some rags. I grabbed all of them and dried myself.

I felt more or less saved for the time being. It was awful to feel dirty like an animal.

The stink diminished but was not gone.

# CHAPTER 9

## DICK'S PHILOSOPHY

I changed my clothes.

I didn't have too many anyway.

I dragged myself to the kitchen to get rid of the terrible stink in my bedroom.

I opened the window and fanned the air with a newspaper.

No way.

Maybe I should demolish the house to get rid of the stink.

Maybe! Who knows?

I was hungry and thirsty, and I didn't know who would ever help me.

Now I felt what was really like being alone in the world. Where was my mom or dad to help me?

I needed them so much.

I started crying.

I felt so lonely.

I even missed Grandpa.

I saw a picture of my mom, and I spat on it. I shouted, "Fucking whores! Don't make children and abandon them."

If I had the power, I'd pass a law sentencing to death all mothers and fathers who abandon their kids.

Kill them all. Yeah, all of them!

No mercy.

---

I had calmed down.

Come to think of it, making children is just a matter of sex in the workings.

Before anything else, there is sex. And I fuck like crazy.

And those chicks, what are they?

They're all stupid whores crazy for cocks.

Long live the holy cock.

The rest is just shit! Just fairy tales!

I felt relieved. Now I knew what life was all about.

A big pile of shit.

When Larry told me, "Hey, Dick, life's nothing. Just a continuous desperate run after cunts," I didn't believe him then.

I didn't care.

---

Yes! Yes! Yes! That's it!

Why should it be like that if you think that all the people are made with the cock.

No scientist has discovered another way!

Actually in our black community, there are many children like me.

Their mothers are fucking like there's no tomorrow and don't give a shit about the string of children they produce.

And I understand that the state has to take care of them.

Why?

Because sex is demanding its rights.

It's now or never, as Presley use to sing. And that's it.

That was what Jessica was saying a few days ago.

I guess she was right.

Absolutely correct.

I was calm, and I had a crazy desire to fuck.

Don't know why, but my dick was getting hard.

My arms and legs were still hurting, but not asmuch as before.

I thought of looking for Hillary and fucking her.

I hadn't seen her in a few days.

She was always ready for it.

She would take my long cock into her hand, kissing it and sucking it and passionately playing with it.

Each time she saw my cock, she was losing it.

I didn't know her last name.

After all that Mr. Jack had told me, I was really curious and perplexed.

Hillary told me that white girls were crazy about black guys with big cocks. They loved it.

Some of them would marry the guys even if they were filthy and poor.

It's true not all black guys have long dicks.

Just some of them.

That's it.

"So get out of the house, you dumb head, and live your life," I said. "Don't shit all over yourself. You're gonna do what Mom and your dad did and all blacks around us do. Nobody can change our very normal way of life."

I went to school for a while. And what?

That's another piece of shit.

The kids came to school to get some free lunch, show off how big their cocks were, and have some fun.

The teacher ladies had the same life. The lonely, single ones were at the mercy of any guy in our black community.

They were very busy getting their pussies fucked every day. That's why any man in our black community was more than welcome.

Living the good life.

One night when I mounted Hillary to fuck her, she stopped and told me frankly, "Why are you men so dirty and smelly and don't take care of yourselves? You got boils of all colors on your ass and around your dick, you're unshaved, your breath smells like shit, and you fart all the time. Some white guys are like this too. We want to fuck, but a little self-care doesn't hurt anyone."

---

In our community, scandals break out all the time.

The police come day and night to stop them from killing one another.

If they don't kill one another today, they'll do it tomorrow for sure.

There are always plenty of reasons to fight.

Many died of gunshots or stabbed like animals or strangled.

It was easier with the chicks. Poor cunts, sometimes I even took pity on them.

Because they were not strong, it was a joke for any black dude to fuck them whenever he felt like.

Even those chicks with huge asses were in danger at any moment.

That was why some of them got pregnant by mistake.

Maybe that's why mothers hate their kids and abandon them with no regrets.

Maybe they got pregnant while being raped.

Everything was okay. Life was going on.

Some wiseass chick would call the cops. She was wasting her time.

Who cared about the alleged rape?

Everything can be arranged.

Mr. Jack told me one day he was going to see a judge to cancel that type of complaints.

So long, smart-ass.

# CHAPTER 10

# THE FUNERAL

The painful and cruel day of the funeral has come.

Too cruel to such a happy family like ours.

Too cruel to a dedicated wife and mother.

And too cruel to us, the two children who fromnow on would only live in pain for losing our dear beloved daddy.

And too cruel to a young, active, and happy man who once was our daddy.

It was very sad to learn and say that now "we don't have a daddy anymore!"

Why?

So that a scared and desperate young black guy shouldn't go to jail after the crimes he committed outof wild jealousy by shooting two other young people, his ex-girlfriend and her new boyfriend, who refused to put the gun down and shot my father right in the left eye from seven feet distance.

A good and experienced policeman who never killed anyone, my father was desperately trying to save lives by putting his life on the line, and he was killed on duty.

In a last effort, he asked the two other policemen not to shoot the young black guy who stubbornly refused to put the gun down.

My father approached the young black guy and begged him to surrender and put the gun for his own good.

He went there confident that logic and reality would make the young black guy listen to his advice and save his life.

Dad spoke directly to the scared young man and tried to persuade him that everything was going to be all right if he put his gun down.

He got to about seven feet from the guy and extended his arm to take the gun.

He didn't threaten or scare him for a second.

Quite the opposite, in a kind voice he told him he had two kids himself and that in life anyone could make a mistake, even his kids.

That moment, the black guy pulled the trigger.

No mercy!

Then he threw the gun and ran away. Simple and decisive!

The criminal bullet went into my dad's left eye, continued straight through his brain, that being soft tissue didn't oppose any resistance, came out of dad's skull, and went so far away that it took the police more than six hours to find it in one the many piles of garbage littering the street.

The internal bleeding and waves of blood gushing out were fatal.

My father died on the spot.

The doctors at the hospital understood the trauma and desperately tried to do everything in their power.

A brain destroyed by such a lethal force cannot be saved.

Ever.

Nobody can.

---

The funeral service was held a week later, and many of my father's colleagues came.

A few thousand.

Those moments made a strong impression on me, and I understood that my dad hadn't died in vain.

Our community's appreciation for him was a big surprise for me.

Thousands upon thousands of people attended, some had come from far away, in order to salute him on his last trip and in recognition of his honest life who upheld the life of young black man and gave his life for that.

It would have been so simple and even legal to shoot the young black.

But he couldn't.

His humanity cost him his life, and he died a violent and unfair death.

I was shocked when the mayor, di Blasio, arrived, and absolutely all the police officers showed him their contempt.

All the police officers turned their back to him and shouted, "You have innocent blood on your hands!"

I was really shocked.

What gives?

The supreme chief arrived, and all the policemen booed him like he was a nobody?

Well, there must be something dirty here.

I'd find out.

I must find out why!

But it was useless.

Daddy left us forever.

Mom was under sedation to help her resist the pain.

George was running from me to Mom and maybe tried to forget the dramatic moment, or maybe he didn't understand true proportions of this tragedy.

His life had changed too.

Very violently changed.

I was desperate, and the horror that my father was really dead gave me cold shivers and unbearable pain.

I wanted to die.

I couldn't take any more suffering.

I was looking at the people around me and asking for some help impossible to find.

I was hoping that Dad was back home, that it was just a passing figment of my imagination, and that life would go on happily for our family.

Thoughts were rushing toward me, going away, and then coming back to me. I was dizzy for enduring so much pain.

I couldn't hear anything around me.

I knew that a lot of police officers spoke nicely about dad and a lot people were crying.

So it was true.

Dad was gone.

Dad died on duty.

You could call it whatever you wanted. For Mom and George and me, it didn't matter anymore.

I was hoping against hope that Dad would come back from a longer mission.

I was howling in pain, and several people tried to soothe me.

I didn't see or hear anything.

I fell down. A few people helped me get up.

I cried out loud, "Dear Daddy, do you really want to leave us? Am I really not going to ever see you again? Please answer me. Dear beloved Daddy, how can you leave without telling us a word? I'm so little, and this world is too big for me! My dear beloved daddy, please tell me, did I do something wrong?

"My dear beloved daddy, you didn't tell me what to do. What do you want me to do in this hard and painful world? Please, Daddy, please come here. I'm waiting for you and can't go home. Without you,

I feel alone now. Please come back to me because I've always been a good boy for you and for Mom."

I was howling in pain.

I couldn't stop crying in desperation. I understood that from now on, nothing was going to be the same.

Why?

The tears of a woman who had taken me into her arms were mixing with my own in a pool of tears.

I was lonely.

Forever.

I was a poor child, fatherless and lonely.

Lonely forever.

My dear beloved daddy didn't even have time to see me for a last time.

From that moment on, I had to suffer and live as my dear beloved daddy would have liked me to live.

Daddy went far away, and I felt very good when I thought about him.

Several times a day I was praying God to take care of him, even though I didn't really understood how things were going on up there.

He had been and still is my role model.

He was a very brave man, a true father to his two sons.

But God took him too soon.

Who could fill my need for him?

I kept thinking, "Why was Dad murdered like an animal? Why was the young black man not at school on the park? Why did he have a firearm in his pocket? Why didn't his parents know what he was doing all by himself? How come that a child actually needed to kill his girlfriend and her new boyfriend so that police would be call in to that place? And why, why did he refuse to put the down the gun for his own good?"

You know, ever since Dad died like a dog in the street, I've been thinking about a lot of things!

Day after day, thoughts are rushing through my mind.

I know! I don't have any clear answers, but I can't help it.

A horrible disaster had fallen upon our family. A long, endless sorrow replaced our happiness forever.

# CHAPTER 11

# TALKING TO MR. GLENN

Years had come and gone one after the other.

I had shed a lot of tears. I was sure not only me.

I was sure of that.

I wasn't myself anymore.

After going to university, my life became more peaceful. I had stuff to do every day.

I received a lot of help from one of daddy's friends, a police officer who had recently been murdered himself like a dog in the middle of the street.

He left two orphan kids, two other innocent victims of a policeman's life.

The Police Department had set up scholarships for the children of police officers killed on duty.

I remember years ago when dad's former coworkers came to visit us, both us and Mom were so proud. They used to say nice things about Dad.

They would bring me pencils and notebooks and many other things. I liked all the different kinds of candy they brought to us. We enjoyed very much the presence of Dad's friends.

One day, when they stepped into our front yard, I was startled and very excited.

One of them looked just like my father.
My sorrow heart started beating like crazy.
I was breathless.
Tears were choking me.
I knew it wasn't him, but what if it was him?
Such a pity!
That was our destiny.

On many occasions while walking in the city, I used to see Dad. I would pray to God to make it possible so that the man was Dad himself.

Again, a heavy sorrow descended on my heart.
Hey! Death is forever.
No exceptions.
Only dreams and hopes and illusions.

---

I understood that we had to live with that great pain in our heart and that I had to take care of Mom.

I knew Dad would have told me that, but his short life on earth didn't allow him to give me any advice.

Mother started seeing another man, also a policeman, but an officer in a higher position.

That man was not going to die in the street like my father. He was sitting at a desk and sending others out in the street to fix the big social problems of the city.

Problems that instead of diminishing were becoming more and more acute and numerous.

---

Mom's life had become a little bit more settled. I was watching over her lovingly and trying to be helpful for her.

She was a woman, and life must go on.

One day she wanted to introduce to me the big boss guy. I couldn't do it, and I asked her not to be mad with me. She was so shy and helpless, and shame overcame her.

I'd never liked that, but I couldn't scold her or stop her.

It was her life, and her need to be with somebody was understandable.

I still loved Dad enormously. Even today, after so many years, I had the impression and the hope that he would come back home.

Back to me!

At least for me. Nobody can understand it!

When somebody tries to stop my dreaming, I feel sad and disheartened. Loving my dad so much, I was expecting Mom to stay home just for me, her child. My eternal respect for Dad made me a bit selfish.

On one of the many visits of dad's friends to our home, I met Mr. Glenn. He seemed to be the most touched and spoke to me in special way.

He was the only one who knew my secret, my unshakable hope that Dad would come back home. He was much impressed with my great love for Dad.

I asked Mr. Glenn why we needed the police, why people were fighting and killing one another, why it was necessary for the police to stand between them and stop them.

What could be done?

He stared at me and tried to explain it to me.

"At first glance, everything doesn't make any sense. It's very complicated. People are different from each other since they are born. Some feel the need to torture and to kill. Others wouldn't kill a fly. Totally different from a million points of view.

"There are others who always need protection, and society created something good. The law. That's it. The law so that everyone must live and act in compliance with the law! Nobody is above the law! Let's just think about it. What kind of society would that be where anyone can do absolutely as they please? What kind of life is that when you get no respect, anybody can break into your home, steal your property, or abuse your loved ones whenever they feel like!

"It is clear that this is not possible and cannot be allowed. Even ancient societies created laws for all their citizens. I guess now you understand why we need a police force. It's for the safety of each and every member of society. Capisco?

"The police force is composed of members of society. They are not supermen. No! Not at all. They are simple citizens with a strong and permanent commitment to help everyone abide by the law. Without law there can be no freedom. Simple as that.

"For multiple reasons and in many situations sometimes hard to understand, some members of society choose not to abide by the law. They don't understand that the law is good surprisingly even for them. But they don't care. They only want to do what they please, not what's good for society. They got no time to philosophize. Then they do things that are hard to understand and even harder to accept.

"Automatically they break the law! And as no law can be ignored, they automatically become police clients!

Why?

Because due to special rules, only police is entitled to protect a person against anyone who tries to encroach on his rights, whatever those rights may be.

When the police have to intervene, it's not an easy job.

It's not a joke.

You can't play games with the police.

There are many good things set in place and many people's lives have been saved. But the world is what it is and don't care too much about that.

Now we're talking about policemen as members of society.

They are like me and you.

They got families, kids. They have their own troubles like everybody else.

They are very courageous people who will go on a mission in dangerous places, day or night, in a house or a place under attack, and they will try all kinds of strategies when confronted with all kinds of wackos.

Whoever has problem, they call the police.

And the police come in a hurry to help themout.

The police helps young kids grow and stay healthy, prevented them from being abducted, abused sexually, or otherwise.

The police protect our mothers, sisters, grandmothers from being raped, humiliated, assaulted, and so on.

The police help us when we are in big trouble in our lives.

The police are permanently watching over social peace and work hard to protect us from wackos, junkies or violent individuals.

They don't get big salaries for the tough job of protecting the rest of us members of society.

Sometimes I think that by putting their lives on the line for us is a sacrifice.

What can I say?

We all need the Police very much and all the time.

Whether we like it or not, it doesn't matter.

But the policemen may be confronted by an enemy at any time. They are in a state of war at all times.

They are the soldiers of a special army, standing between us and our enemies.

No price is too high to protect us, and many lose their lives on duty.

They are our living heroes we must respect them!

Now you know how many police officers die in action. Their life will never be easy, and that's why not everyone can become a policeman.

Their mad courage, their passionate wish to help people in trouble, and their supreme sacrifice are all fascinating, and I think we ought to respect them and do as they tell us to do.

Their work is not like ball dancing or a walk in the park. They have to save lives as soon as possible. They have to help in emergency situations.

In order to fulfill their tough policing job, society must help them. Police officers need encouragement, appreciation, respect, and celebration of their accomplishments.

Without that, policemen would be shy, undecided, confused, and eventually inefficient. A lot of people will lose because of that.

A police force intentionally kept under fear and pressure and threatened with harsh penalties or loss of their job is a situation that works against the interests of our society.

Nowadays, we police officers live through hard, bitter, and unfair times under OBAMA's regime.

In order to have the black population responding to any call to go out onto the streets, he gave them anything they wanted and started a heinous program of discrediting and destroying us.

We know that this total war against the police force that started from very high up and without any real explanation only brings more trouble and pain to society.

The higher-ups need the blacks to keep them in power. That's why the police is a good example for them to show how much they care about the blacks.

Pretty soon we have presidential elections coming, and we expect more and more trouble against us in the police force.

The Justice Department started to work under the command of the White House and all government departments are involved.

But the worst is Holder, formerly head of DOJ, now under Loretta Lynch.

Police officers in most critical situations desperately try to make the best decisions.

Unintended mistakes are made in any workplace.

No police officer in the entire American police force wants such complicated and desperate situations where you have to shoot or hit somebody!

They are good citizens.

They want to help the innocent escape dangers and calm things down.

Honesty, policemen don't need other troubles. They have enough already.

But when the higher-ups yell racism because a police officer shot and killed in self-defense a black man. The police officer was insulted, humiliated simply for doing his job. That's too much. Enough is enough.

The result is a weak, shy, and inefficient police force.

It's not good when the higher-ups suggest and launch slogans like "Cops are stupid," "Cops are racist," or "Death to cops" without a real trial in a court of justice under the existing laws.

Shame on those who seek to encourage violence, heinous crimes, social chaos, and finally injustice. The consequences of their actions are fast coming, and innocent people are already paying the price.

Why favor one against others?

In Ferguson, Baltimore, Chicago, New York, and other places, the crime wave is getting unexpectedly high. It's getting awfully high!

Even blacks that need protection are dying in droves.

Because they kill one another for their higher-up bosses.

A lot of police officers got the message to avoid police involvement, to stay away from violent cases of any kind. However, the consequences are painful.

Crime and violence of all kind statistics are alarmingly high.

See the recent crime committed in New York against the niece of a well-known black man. Many other crimes will happen as long as the police force is paralyzed.

That's why the war against the police force concocted by the clever OBAMA, by Holder, Al Sharpton, and Mayor di Blasio is a total war against us all honest, law-abiding citizens.

We already know that OBAMA is seriously thinking about a new mandate as president.

It's damn easy for him!

It's a joke for him to get a new one!

He's been relentlessly bringing in millions of black Africans, millions of Latinos, Muslims tone or million. He's been releasing hundreds of thousands of criminals from jails, saying they were wrongly convicted, and now accepting people to vote without asking for their ID, claiming that would be discrimination. The job is almost done.

Right there he's got about 50 percent of the votes in his favor.

I asked, "What do you mean without ID?"

It's hard to believe that in today's America, there might be individuals who live without electricity, heating, TV, radio, car, money, bank account, magazines, family doctors, hospital, and so on. That's why you need an ID for your own good.

Anyway, it's not difficult to get one. You can get it real fast.

Is there anyone in America living like in a third world country?

Or maybe isolated in a cave or in the mountains?

Even if there was one individual like that, the authorities with their millions of civil servants can solve that right away.

That's on one hand.

Supposedly they know all those who don't have an ID.

On the other hand.

They can go to those who don't have ID and get them a nice brand-new one on the spot! You know how they go to old retired people's homes and give them an ID to benefit from reductions on public transportation?

They take their picture right there, and in a couple of days, the retirees receive their ID card by mail.

Or when they go to voting stations with all their revolutionary enthusiasm and without any ID, they could take their cool picture and issue on the spot an ID.

But they don't care about anything. What ID card? But how can you deny them their right to vote?

Especially for the president?

Hypothetically, if an American citizen does not have ID card, that constitutes a great embarrassment for the Democrats, for the Republicans, for the government, and generally for the Department of Justice.

It's so easy to help them get one that you wonder how is it possible not to have one?

Ha, ha!

---

Mr. Glenn replied, "I don't think it's possible in this day and age not to have an ID card."

But Nancy, that millionaire with her private jet, said, "No! We can't give up the votes of tens of thousands of people who don't have an ID card. That is pure discrimination. Why wouldn't you allow them to vote?"

And all the Democrats burst into tears on cue!

"Please don't deprive them of their right to vote. To vote for us, of course."

Without an ID, they will make and effort and vote many times.

It's not really difficult to do that without an ID.

Police have already arrested many individuals for voting fraud.

I'm sure they are on OBAMA's list for fast release.

They deserve it, don't they?

Eric, also called Holder, chipped in quickly, "Hold on, you know my name is Holder. Justice is mine. I'll get a few tens of thousands of votes in a jiffy."

Unfortunately, the new chief of justice, one Lynch, Loretta, categorically said that we cannot deprive tens of thousands of people of their right to vote just because they got no ID card.

That's real discrimination!

Really!

So that the Liberal scam goes on.

"Those Republicans are so stupid!"

Mr. Glenn continued, "That thing with Hillary is a bad joke. There's a big problem with Benghazi and the secret emails."

Honestly, Hillary has no real chance.

However, it must be fascinating being a president as long as Hillary at her very advanced age desperately tries to get such a position. May be she wants to be the Grandma of American People.

It seems me very strange. She was unable to protect the four American people in huge political position in Libya.

So how will she really protect more than three hundred million American people? American people!

Even if she got more than six hundred of desperate petitions for help from the American ambassador in Libya, she decided to ignore all of them.

Consequently the American ambassador in Libya and other three American people were killed due to a terrorist attack long, long, long, long time planned and very well-known.

Else after that she lied about everything is other shit.

She is totally out of logic and skills.

Not to mention her and OBAMA's "great success" in terms of Arabian Spring!

So for what she did not do for the four American people she must be arrested and convicted for deliberate crime.

But she wants to be rewarded with a special, undeserved position as president of America.

If she would be a lady, then she would start a long period of silence and hot prayers to GOD!

How could some American people not realize the drama she created and to stop her easily?

I think that any honest and loving the right American citizen never ever will vote for her!

Now OBAMA wants to trick Biden to take part in the election circus.

You know, the guy who blunders each time he opens his mouth. I guess he's nothing but a joker.

The man with the classic jobs in three letters.

He won't get 10 percent because he's so compromised. He could be OBAMA No. 2 if he was elected!

Thank God he decided not to run!

The devious OBAMA knows exactly well.

It's just a distraction. He already gave Biden his blessing, although it's not fair to Hillary.

The smart OBAMA threw a monkey wrench into the opposition's works.

Didn't he say some time ago, "I like to be the president of America. If I ran for re-election, I would certainly win a third mandate."

And with shy tone of voice, he added, "But the Constitution doesn't allow me to do it."

Bullshit!

What Constitution?

The American Constitution means nothing to him. The entire USA knows how many times OBAMA shamelessly breached the Constitution.

For him there is no Constitution. He' got clear and precise ideas how to grab power again by any means possible.

Isn't it great to be president of the Unites States and practically do whatever you like? He always acts like an emperor. And who's going to stop him from becoming a real emperor? And who's going to stop him from staying an emperor for life?

The plan has been made for a long time. Just watch and see.

The blacks will always fight for him and will support him no matter what.

And he will reward them by giving them all that the whites possess until the whites are completely eliminated.

We have our sources that tell us that the smart OBAMA doesn't give a damn on the American Constitution. Or the white or even the blacks.

He just wants power and he will surely get it.

Soon.

The police will be annihilated so that the white population will have no protection in case of a social riot that is planned to start soon.

The new slogan Black Lives Matter is absurd and has no logic but that's another story.

You heard that saying, "The end justifies the means." That's it.

God help America!

Because it has never been in such an imminent danger as it is today.

Hussein OBAMA will give a short order, "All blacks in the street, the great day has come. Break and vandalize. Set cars on fire. And shooting days and nights."

The policemen will just step aside because they are already scared by the racism label and will not try to opposite it in any way.

Nobody will be protected!

Even the policemen will be attacked with stones and bottles and will be totally paralyzed so as not to forget about racism.

After a few days of chaos, the white people's fear of death will overwhelm them. Smoke in the streets and apprehension for what else may be coming.

With all the police cars on fire, with no chance to defend themselves, absolutely the entire America will ask for Hussein OBAMA's help, just as planned.

And in a very difficult sole moment, he will come in and solve the problem he created in the first place.

We should feel blessed and happy and should kneel in front of him imploring him to make peace in America.

At this point, Hussein Barack OBAMA together with all his court prepared in advance shall appear on all TV channels and shall declare a coup d'état.

He will ask all the viewers for a new and long mandate as president of America.

Of course, with this special emergency situation, he will dissolve the government and the Senate and will suspend the American Constitution that in all honesty used to give him a lot of headaches.

Done!

The chaos in America is resolved. All the blacks should go back to the barracks, sorry, I mean to their houses.

Simple, efficient, and very cheap.

Who could oppose it?

He was begged, implored to save the nation!

Many white women, who only want black cock any way, will stand by their black husbands.

The white men are tired and disorganized. They come from work, water the lawn, watch some TV, and doze on the couch. And the same routine the next day!

That is how if the police force is dead, OBAMA becomes the new emperor.

And then we'll see the consequences and troubles.

Yes!

Anything is possible.

Do not minimize it.

Defend yourselves right now.

Defend America!

What I said may seem exaggerated, but such a scenario is possible at any time.

You'll see!

# CHAPTER 12

## ERIC

I met Mr. Jack soon.

He was looking for me too.

He had something special and good for a fucking black guy, as he like to say.

We went to get something to eat because I don'twhy, but I was always hungry.

We were eating in a hurry. Mr. Jack took out apicture of an ugly black boy.

"Do you know this dude? No?"

I stopped munching and took an attentive lookat the picture.

Hm.

That was Eric, the classroom clown.

"What about him? He's a good boy."

Mr. Jack said, irritated, "A good boy? Damn this good boy. He's a big black idiot."

I said, "Yeah, he was not too smart in school, but he was doing good business with drugs, chicks to fuck, and good, cheap second stuff recently stolen from different places."

I remember one a black guy also from a black community came over, and they chatted for hours.

I didn't fucking understand why they talked so much.

I called him to come play a basketball game 'cause we didn't have enough players.

He furiously yelled back at me "Nigger, can't you see I'm busy?" and went away with the other guy.

"Shut the fuck up and eat," said Mr. Jack. "I see you got a big mouth, boy. The problem with this idiot is that he works undercover for the police. And I don't like it. I don't like at all. Not a bit.

"I can tell you a secret now. A big secret. "This guy used to work for me and knows lots of stuff about me. "He was promoted to the position of manager for Special Actions Against Whites. The southwest area."

"How could I find out if he ratted out to the police? Honestly, I think he did. I don't know for sure, sure. I guess you understand why I called you here urgently. If needed, we'll eliminate him in a flash. One less moron. Who cares about him? Actually, he doesn't have any family, too. Just like you."

I gulped the rest of my food and said, "What do you want me to do? That guy didn't even talk to me. When he sees me, he yells, 'Nigger, did you see your momma?' Don't forget to fuck her on my behalf when you catch her. He knows I live alone just like him, but he likes to tease me all the time. I sure don't like this guy either. So tell me what to do. You know he's big. But his prick is so small I once chided him, and he chased me for a mile to beat me. Man, he beat the shit outa me. I'll never forgive him for that."

Now really ticked off, Mr. Jack cut me short.

"Fuck you with your stupid fucking stories. I got big problems, and you bug me with these stupid things?

"So what if his cock is small. Good for you got a big one. Damn you stupid blacks you think of nothing but fucking. Whites are right when they treat you like idiots. Anyway, what can we do? The higher-up bosses want action not something else. They don't give a shit about you and your dirty sex. Do what they us to do. They'll take care of the rest. They'll make sure you're not hungry."

A few minutes later, Mr. Jack became a bit friendlier and told me clearly in a softer voice, "Go make this guy your buddy. Take fifty dollars and buy him. If this works, I'll give you more dough, a lot more.

"Spy on everything he says and does. What his friends are, where he sleeps, who he fucks, and what he thinks about me. I know it's a lot of stuff all of a sudden, but you gotta try."

He paid for the meal and handed me nineteen dollars for expenses.

When he took the money out of his pocket, I was stunned.

Mr. Jack was a millionaire for sure.

He was always sharply dressed, slender, very black, a mean black with a pair of large prescription glasses that were always dirty.

Mr. Jack took my arm and told me straightforward, "Listen, boy, I really need you. Don't try to disappear again because I'll cut your balls off. When I send for you, make sure you come right away. You gotta come here fast. Otherwise, you're gonna be in big trouble. You don't fuck with me."

Suddenly the guy shouted at me, scaring everyone around us.

But Mr. Jack didn't care about anything.

He had tons of money. I'd never seen so money in my life. He had good connections high up there in the government, and now I understood that his power in our community was greater than the one of an African tribal chief.

"Do you get it?" He was shouting at me and gripping my arm so hard I almost yelled in pain.

I smiled, and I thought it was a joke.

But I quickly understood that from then on I was Mr. Jack's property.

I was really scared, and I figured I was in deep shit and that in our black community, a black dude's life means nothing.

Yeah, brother.

He told me a lot of stories about blacks killing whites, but in the end, he came to fuck me, a black guy just like him.

I didn't know what to believe anymore.

Are the whites our enemies that we must kill soon, or do you blacks in the black community want to use us as your slaves for your own interests?

I realized why Mr. Jack was not married.

He didn't need to.

He was the one fucking whoever he wanted.

All the chicks were afraid of him.

I was dumbfounded when I heard that he even fucked the married girls, with or without the knowledge of their boyfriends or husbands.

I started to dislike Mr. Jack.

He was a shitty, lying black guy.

He was a big piece of shit.

But black.

Was this the guy who would help the higher-ups to kill all the whites?

Now I didn't understand anything.

Holy cow!

I needed a fix again.

It was good. I still got two in that box under the bed.

I couldn't believe the fucking shit I got myself into.

Couldn't screw around with Mr. Jack.

I was fucked.

Again I felt I missed my mom and dad, my grandma, and even my grandpa.

It was so tough to be alone.

Alone in the world.

Many tears started rolling down my cheeks.

# CHAPTER 13

## BILL AND MARK

On my way to the library, I met Mark, sort of a friend of mine.

His father was a big boss with the Liberals.

"Hi, Mark!"

"Hi, Bill!"

"How are you? I'm sure everything is fine. Are you coming to the Forensic Science course today? A renowned professor is giving the lecture. I want to hear him. Too many crimes and social problems in our city. Seems worse than ever. There have always been murders, rapes, burglaries, and whatnot. But now, since OBAMA and his men started the total war against police, it's worse than ever."

"Absolutely! It's like the world is going crazy. How couldn't it be?" said Bill. "The police force is intimidated, humiliated, and anyone can make fun of them. Cops! These are the people we sacrifice, people who for a few dollars are exposed to situations that really make you pity them! Do you think it's easy to go to the crime scene and try to calm down all kinds of crazies? They are fighting and killing each other like there's no tomorrow, and you a poor cop are trying to help them?"

"How?" asked Mark. "What do you mean poor? These guys are trained and know how to act in any situation. Look at their muscles. You don't kid around with them, bro."

"Oh my, that was in the past," replied Bill.

"Now the terror against the police makes the entire police force impotent. The fear of being thrown in prison by some Liberal in power, like that crazy bitch in Baltimore, mayer, or to be threatened with losing your job and being dropped like a piece of garbage, losing your meager pension after so many years of hard work, you really don't know what to do. Every morning, before going on patrol, the police chief always scares you. Not to mention the horror that some wacko is going to kill you and leave your kids and family alone and helpless."

---

It takes a very special person to decide to become a police officer.

There are probably a few things attracting them to apply for such a job.

I for one, you could give me the world, and I wouldn't work as a policeman.

I shiver only when I think about it.

I know there is a great need for them.

Who would prevent regular people from becoming innocent victims of some crazy guy?

In the end, man is a beast.

Whether white or not, it's the same.

Mark said, "Why are so many blacks in prison? When OBAMA said that 'there are more blacks in prison that in school,' I thought it was just propaganda."

"But it's true." Bill added, "I've always asked myself why was my father shot like an animal and butchered with a knife beyond recognition? Where does this hate and power come to kill a policeman on duty? Without any fear of the consequences? Why? Why didn't they obey the order to put down their guns? You know, ever since my father died in the street shot like a dog, I've been thinking a lot."

Mark said, "Life goes on. "Stop tormenting yourself now."

I replied, "No! I can't stop thinking. You would do the same."

---

This way, I learned many things.

More than 3,500 years ago, ancient Egyptians were very much involved in buying and selling slaves.

The institution of slavery in Africa existed long, long time ago.

This slavery was practiced across Africa from prehistoric times to the modern era.

For menial work or domestic labor, people used slaves!

You will be very surprised to find about white slaves!

Between 1520 and 1800, over 1.5 million of European Christians were enslaved by Muslims of the Barbary Coast in North Africa!

Slaves were still slaves. It didn't matter. They were whites or blacks.

Buying or selling slaves were regular jobs in countries along the Nile River.

By the way slavery was one of the oldest trades well known to people.

To be honest, all races and all civilizations have practiced it: China, India, Arabs, Africa, Europe, and in the Americas.

White peoples are not exceptions!

Julius Caesar asked to send over 1 million white slaves for the Roman Empire!

I am really very surprised and shocked how millions of European or Egyptian descendants of whites slaves or some blacks slaves from France, Spain, Egypt, and others countries never ever asked reparation from the Italian state for these slaves that one day were sent by Julius Caesar to Rome to perform hard work or to be gladiators.

Not any kind of great or nice demonstrations or to kill with a bestial hatred hundreds of innocent white policemen during their duties.

Sure they understood the ridicule to keep guilty innocent people for not having the slightest contribution at what happened long, long time ago!

---

The Muslims were probably the world's largest enslavers, and an estimated twenty-one million people become the victims of Islamic across Barbarian costs.

The modern slaves in England and New World, kids in slavery, took them from orphanages or work-houses and put to work for a lifetime of horrors daily over sixteen hours, no breaks, and when trying to sleep a little being so tired, they were whipped awake.

And mutilated for life during this hard work, these kids were simply turned out onto the street.

Slaves in America were often better off than white workers in North America!

Between AD 600 and AD 1900, Muslims enslaved between twelve and twenty million Africans.

I am puzzled why France did not ask reparation from Italy for the slavery times of millions of white slaves that Julius Caesar sent them to Rome!

So a millennium of long sufferings, hard lives, and humiliations for these unlucky people that had become slaves!

Muslims, whites, blacks, or so were obliged to be slaves in some way or other!

Nobody asked them if they want or not!

The power and force were the only answer for them that time.

Honestly I do not like or want to offend anyone.

I dare say that we have to respect the memories of all the innocent people that sometimes worked and lived across history like slaves!

And I think it's correct to talk when we talk about the long time of slavery about them too!

Why ignore other slaves in favor of others?

All deserved a little respect.

We love to talk desperately about the discrimination!

Please stop discriminating them forever!

Being a slave must be terrible, and when European countries decided around 1800 to abolish slavery, many African states sent special representatives to oppose to these laws!

They asked firmly to let them, African people, with slaves because they thought this was their business!

---

The blacks in America came here to work and help with the harvests and whatnot.

They didn't come because they wanted to.

They hadn't even heard of America.

They were captured by the whites and brought to America and sold as slaves.

Many others were sold as slaves by their African slave masters.

It's awful to be a slave. It's not good.

Some of them had a hard life, others a better one. According to everyone's luck.

You know the history of America.

It's full of stories like that.

Those who brought them here, those whites or blacks, are just a bunch of criminals.

Oh! I would dig them out of their graves and kill them all again!

They really deserve it!

How can you force some primitive, innocent people to leave their family, their customs and traditions, their games and their dances, their loves, and their carefree lives and bring them to a foreign, hostile, and cold place where they didn't belong at all.

How much suffering, desperation, and fear in their pure souls.

After all, they were all just big children.

If you put yourself in their place just for a second, you would be horrified.

But times goes on.

No one can stop it.

Willy-nilly they started a new and harsh life in a world that wasn't theirs.

It's true that some slaves tried to run away and be liberated, but they were quickly caught and brought back to submission.

You know, I've learned a lot in school.

But the things I found out by myself are different.

By the way!

Did you see the blacks in the street?

How loud they speak, how noisy and agitated they are.

They are always like that.

A high school history teacher, a black woman friend of mine, opened my eyes.

Because of the huge stress they lived under here for years and years, black people have changed a lot.

In their hearts, they have a big and permanent racial complex.

A big and hard-to-bear sentiment of inferiority.

Nothing in the world will ever change that.

They couldn't change their slave status, and then they understood that submission is theirs.

The hate in their hearts kept growing and growing.

Sincerely, they are right.

But hold on!

Their liberation coming as a result of whites' struggle does not count?

Nothing can change their state of mind.

And many don't like the fact they are different from the whites.

They are all the time under the impression that someone is out there to humiliate them, minimize them, treat them as secondhand citizens, that there someone is always trying to discredit them cheat them or take their rights away.

Some of them thought that they are the filth of America, and the lack of self-respect almost disappears. A huge feeling of defense and pride overcomes them when they think or it seems they are neglected or that someone is trying to take something form them or keep them apart.

If you talk nicely to a black guy, no problem, he's yours.

You got him.

They need the whites' respect and appreciation all the time, almost in everything they do.

Good or bad, it doesn't matter.

They suffer enormously and sometimes can very easily become violent for the smallest reason.

Among the whites, they demand total respect and appreciation.

Did you see how many books in school are about racism?

You'd be surprised what a big difference in behavior, what a huge change when they are among blacks like them.

That's when they really feel good, free, powerful, real bosses.

Living for so many years together in city slums, they have the occasion to really relax.

There is no law here.

No restrictions.

It's just them, no one else.

The fear of police arresting them or putting them in jail doesn't exist here.

Every day there are numerous crimes, fights, threats, unjustified beatings, and abuses of all kinds.

The police is always called.

In their community, some even have power over the others.

The black community is large and always growing.

There are some very well connected high up, and they organize them to come out in the street for real or imaginary rights when needed.

They don't have jobs, so what?

The higher-ups give them food, housing, TVs, cars, and recently phones.

That is why they don't need a job or school or too much education.

Murders, burglaries, and rapes are growing too.

Look at Chicago, Baltimore, Ferguson, New York, and so on.

When they came out and rioted in Baltimore, OBAMA accused the Republicans of cutting some funds of the billions allocated.

Isn't it nice to get billions just for living in the slum?

Years ago, police used to come.

Even if they didn't solve many things, at least they were feared a little bit.

Just the sound of the police siren made you think hard before doing anything stupid. That was still something.

Ever since the Total War against Police, the police don't go there anymore.

The big bosses need their votes real bad.

Without their votes, they lose their power, and they can't accept that.

Do you really think OBAMA would have seen the inside of the White House without the millions of blacks waiting in huge lines to vote for him?

No way!

The fact that he didn't do too much is another story.

Unemployment among the black minority has risen to over 25 percent, and the future doesn't look promising!

OBAMA, the liar, knows it but keeps saying it's only 5.1 percent.

But OBAMA is smart. You don't need too much brain to quickly understand how one can benefit from that.

Lacking any kind of experience, with a job nobody ever heard in America of community organizer, without any real education, he quickly understood that the blacks have helped him and will help him.

You can always count on them.

Of course, that sounds like obvious corruption, but who cares.

Agitators like Al Sharpton and many others are making good money.

That's why they have to get out in the street and shout all kinds of slogans, break into businesses, vandalize stores, and steal as much as possible.

Invade the whites.

Scare who?

Isn't it clear?

The whites.

The higher-up blacks in the government need these riots.

Let there be as many blacks in the street as possible.

It doesn't matter that some of the slogans like the one in Ferguson "Don't stop me! Don't shoot!" are obvious fakes.

The blacks have to shout something.

You gotta inflame them, make them feel important fighters, proud defenders of a just cause, what the hell.

The higher-up bosses are not sitting idle.

Now they came up with a new slogan lacking any logic: Black Lives Matter.

Even statistics show how fake it is.

Only 11 percent think that is correct.

While All Lives Matter is 75 percent.

The fact that life is the same for everyone is not important.

They have a whole lot of rights and nobody is trying to take them away.

But they have to be ready to get out in the street when ordered to do so.

Just wait and see whole crowds of black people coming out for revolution from now on.

Presidential elections are coming soon.

Is it true that the higher-up bosses need to hold on to power?

Honestly the higher-up bosses don't have too much consideration for them.

They are just interested in using them when they need it.

And now they do.

That's all.

---

Mark stared at me and said, "Hm."

He's quite clever.

Sure he is.

My dad used to tell my mom about black people being mobilized at an order.

But the higher ups, it wasn't enough to call them.

You have to give them something in return.

The hate against the poor whites, who are already being totally bossed around, must inflame the blacks.

There are plenty of reasons.

When confronted by blacks with guns who fear nothing, some terrified police officers shoot in self-defense.

That's a good thing for the higher-up bosses.

Well, it's clear.

They see it and Dixit.

There is racism in America.

A lot of racism.

We have to stop it by any means possible.

And you black people are called to stop it.

Racism is only against us.

What racism? Of course there no such danger."

But the higher-up bosses must give them some explanation and lie to them so they come out against the whites.

The whites must never forget they must pay up for the times long ago when the blacks were slaves.

I don't like all blacks.

But I am not a racist at all.

I have a lot of black friends.

And I appreciate them for their qualities.

They are people like us.

The mistakes of the past were not right.

But it was the whites who set them free and made equal to the whites.

There will always be differences between whites and blacks.

We can't just distort reality.

Lying and lying is not good for anybody.

It doesn't matter the color.

They have rights and nobody intends to take them away.

I will elect a white or a black whenever required.

But that doesn't mean the black must disappear or be marginalized just because he is black!

And I've never thought of discriminate against them.

They are truly very different from us.

No question about it.

But recognizing this is not racism at all.

It's even good.

Knowing that, all of us white and black can work together to make less mistakes to one another.

That is good!

# THE DEATH PENALTY FOR KARL MARX

Mark said, "Don't forget, all populations have their idiots. Their own idiots, of course."

I continued, "The blacks are people too and they have to live. The true discrimination against them comes from the higher-up bosses. We the whites and the blacks have absolutely no reason to fight. What was done is done. It was long time ago. Anyway, they are different. Even OBAMA's Baptist pastor, a guy names Jeremiah Wright, who baptized his children or something, said and demonstrated that blacks learn and think differently from whites, that there is something with the black people's brain. I watched him attentively on TV. I don't think that guy was labeled a racist."

---

We were discussing so intently we didn't even feel time flying.

We were getting ready to go to classes when a voice I knew called us.

"Hold on, don't move! Hands up or you gonna be in trouble."

Jimmy came toward us.

"Hi, guys. What were you discussing so seriously? Philosophy?"

Jimmy was a close friend.

He was very intelligent.

This guy really knew everything going on in the department.

The magic eye.

No kidding!

He was the editor of the student's magazine!

Anyway.

He exceled in everything.

You couldn't screw around with him. He'd catchyou right away.

He spoke with an astronomical speed. You could hardly follow him.

And he knew so many jokes you could laugh your pants off when he told them.

His problem was he used foul language.

Out of three words, two were obscenities.

We advised him in a friendly way to change hisstyle.

It was useless.

That was how he is.

Take it or leave it!

He shot straight from the hip.

He didn't care.

But after you'd get to know him, you wouldn't even notice it anymore.

He was cultured and intelligent, and each of us would like to have his sharp and fast mind.

"Hi, faggots," said Jimmy. "What did you fuck recently? Nothing, nothing! Still jerking off? You guysafter so much jerking you are going to get chronic masturbitis. And you know you can only cure that with an infusion of sixteen-year-old pussy, taken three times a day, and it's quite expensive, dude. Do you know that joke with the mouse who got married to a giraffe? Noooo?

"Listen up. This little mouse got married to a giraffe lady. And she was very virgin! A month later, he met a friend. 'What happened to you, dude? I almost didn't recognize you. What's the problem? You have lost a lot of weight. You look scrawny. I've never seen you that skinny. Is she cheating on you? Does she starve you? What's wrong?'

"The little mouse said, 'She's a good girl, she lets me fuck her whenever I want, she even cooks. I can't blame her for anything.'

"'Then what is it?'

"'You know, I'm kind of ashamed to say it. But I'll tell you.'

"'Come on, say it.

"'You know, it's good when I fuck her, but when I want to kiss her, I have to run all the way up her neck to her mouth and then back, and it goes on like that the entire night!'

"'You know? That's it.'

"At this point, his friend said, 'You're such a moron. You should kiss where you fuck.'"

We started laughing hysterically.

That was a good one.

Suddenly Jimmy said in a loud voice, "Let's get serious. What were you talking about? Troubles? Spit it out. Spill the beans, and your buddy will help you."

"Well, we were seriously discussing about the police that under OBAMA's fashionable Total War Against Police lost their power and interest in doing their duty like before. And that's why we see all the troubles. And everybody suffers."

"Listen, kids," said Jimmy. "The trouble with the one up there, not God, but the black guy who was brought to power by blacks and whites is a well-known thing by now. Racism is a big fake or fad. You can call it what you want, it's still shit. It's the creation of some black dudes who are crazy to get some white pussy but also power. Where is the racism?

"Baldwin is black. Long Island is coming right behind it. In Queens and everywhere else, there is plenty of them. Full of blacks. And you should see the cars they bought and drive. And tons of money. They are first in line to be given a job, and nobody, absolutely nobody has refused them anything for over one thousand years. Now the whites have to take care. And now they the blacks are very proud of their origin and mention this hard and up.

"Firstly they are African, and later, later they are American to make clear distinction about we the whites, which are only Americans, and them, it seems to me that they just wants to bring to our attention they are black like an warring to let us, the modest whites, that they are other potential living country any time they like. They must live. Just like us whites. Honestly, I don't see any problem.

"When you switch on the TV, what do you see? Blacks with all kinds of news and games and shows and stories. I don't think there are whites there anymore. Maybe one who lost his way. And what about this."

Normal.

"The Americans brought them to America, so they must make room for them. And they do. Without any problem. People may not like one or he is ugly or he stinks, it's possible. Come on. It's normal. How many people don't like me and can't stand me? And you can see I'm white. It will always be like that. You like someone and you dislike someone else. So what? Can you change the world?

"Even if OBAMA in his hate of white people passed a law saying you have to kiss any black guy's ass if ordered, it would not change anything. Just today I met my good buddy Joshua. He's as black as they come. So what? Girls are crazy to fuck him.

"He told me once he didn't even have time for school. His fucking schedule is full from dawn to dusk. And he fucks only the whitest girls you can get. Therefore, if OBAMA's discriminated blacks fuck all the white cunts, where is the racism? Maybe OBAMA wants to fuck those dumbass white men too.

"What racism, bro? Yesterday I saw, for the hundredth time, a mixed family of a white guy and a black girl. And two little brownies in tow. So? It's the way of life. Darwin explained it clearly about the human species. Fight for Existence? So?

"Smart guys, these black boys. If you look around, you see all the white girls fucking and marrying blacks in droves. Powell, Bush's general, said it better. Take it easy! Very soon around 2050, you won't see any whites in America. Trust me! He said it.

"You're saying the boss high up declared Total War Against American Police? You know what, this OBAMA is a big racist. Being so inefficient in everything he does? He played the racism card hard. So that people let him do what he wanted. In his desperation to fuck America, even in his first inaugural speech, he said some tall tales bigger than his crooked cock.

"He said, 'America is composed first of Muslims. Then Christians and so on.' What Muslims are you talking about, man? America was made by thousands upon thousands maybe millions of Scots and Italians and all kinds of people who fled Europe because of poverty. It's no wonder.

"How much education does this OBAMA have? He wouldn't know. His entire education is that type of quotas for minorities. They even blessed him with the title of professor.

"Poor guy! He can't even speak English correctly. A little better now after talking so much shit continuously. The laughing stock of the world. The smart OBAMA, when not reading the teleprompt, can't even say three words of his own.

"It's true that presently there are lots of Muslims. OBAMA brought in a lot of them. Anyway in 2009, there were not so many as today. Everybody understood what's coming next. His hate of America is great, just like that screw up Giuliani, former mayor of New York, says that OBAMA hates America. The man was sincere. Well! Now he's got the guts. He's retired. And what a nice, fat pension he has, my man."

A lot of people believe OBAMA was not born in America.

That he is a Muslim to the core.

It was said he was born in Kenya.

A lot of Muslim schooling from dawn to dusk in Indonesia, funny relations with American terrorists like his good friend and former English teacher from Chicago, and so on.

What do you want from poor him?

Blood is thicker than water.

Just like they say in Luke's and Matthew's Gospels.

And you want him to love America?

Forget it.

Never.

But he likes to feel important.

This guy loves power more than all American presidents together.

Although he does stupid things and damage and dirties everything with him big smile, his craving for absolute power is something else.

He's got a clear and undeclared creed.

In a covert manner, he wants to make sure that he, OBAMA, did his best to have America totally subjugated, destroyed, and impoverished.

But he was right!

Didn't he declare honestly during the election campaign that he wants to remake America?

OBAMA never said he wanted a strong, rich, and respected America.

Everywhere he went in his wanderings, he abjectly humiliated America.

So what do you expect?

He was very frank when he said that America is first and foremost a Muslim country.

That was exactly what he wanted to remake America.

---

His diabolical plan is working slowly but surely.

Trillions of dollars in debt, more than all other presidents combined, weakening of the armed forces, cowardly and unjustifiably releasing the five terrorists and others before in exchange for a deserter because supposedly "We don't leave no one behind," the millions of immigrants brought in and advised to stay because soon he was going to give a general amnesty even though it was illegal, the millions of

# THE DEATH PENALTY FOR KARL MARX

African blacks coming as visitors and as staying, all treaties clearly signed to the America's disadvantage, his desperation not to trouble his Muslims inviting themto expensive and useless and totally unjustified meetings, all these speak for themselves. And his efforts to help Iran acquire the atomic bomb, they are all clear proof of his hate of America.

How can you allow a country get the atomic bomb when they shout, "Down, America! Death to America!"

Providing pitiful solutions, such as the idea that the world terrorists need jobs even in America.

He has never said anything about Muslim fanatics.

He considered ISIS a bunch of amateurs like kids playing with toys and made sure that nobody bothered them.

---

Well, now Arabians making fun of America is no surprise!

Well, it is normal?

How the Iranian government arrested American sailors, clearly they were in international waters, for strange reasons.

Then they humiliated the American government, who obliged it publicly and was very quick to apologize, and the USA government did it fast, very fast!

There is no more huge and big humiliation for America.

One day the most respected country in the world, now humiliated like a third or fourth country in the world.

Yes, this is a huge and resounding success for OBAMA.

Anyway, it's not about a war or something else.

Really, too much humiliation for us American people obliged to have a president like OBAMA!

For the millions of blacks from Africa who came here as permanent tourists, life is good.

It takes only two minutes for any African to get a US visa.

In order to get a European visa, it takes at least two to six years, and sometimes they don't get it.

Even Hillary Clinton did her best to keep the Europeans in Europe!

How about releasing on the streets tens of thousands of criminals who are already starting to perpetrate abominable crimes against American citizens?

How about his wish to help illegal immigrants settle for a good life in hundreds of American cities under the protection of authorities?

Well, these immigrants must pretty soon pay their dues.

Go and vote for sweet baby OBAMA, the biggest racist that America has ever seen!

How about his desperate struggle to free from jail all kinds of criminals that even the submissive Congress couldn't approve, like the scam with that Mumia Abu-Jamal, who shot in the head for no reason a white policeman.

Right in front of his wife, and so on.

And the fight against justice that supposedly made a mistake by convicting too many to go to jail.

For what?

For drugs?

"But he even confessed by mistake that he had taken drugs enthusiastically all his childhood.

Now he regrets saying it, but it's a bit late!

America will always be under siege of the millions of blacks that when ordered by OBAMA's professional agitators to come out and provoke anarchy.

And he keeps going on relentlessly.

Well!

This foolishly patient America is clouded by many troubles.

I think that the police should understand that any police officer killing by the blacks is an act of war and should be treated as such.

If, God forbid, the police lose this war, then America is doomed.

When the blacks were enslaved, there was white terror, and now is black terror?

It certainly wasn't good then and can't be good now.

All people in the United States of America must have the right to live and must be helped to live in peace.

Peace is better than anything else.

War is not good at all!

---

Based on his hatred for America and abusing the American democracy as no one did before, OBAMA started a special program to null of whites through changing of their culture and American traditions.

A very clear special program to negate American history.

A program that in the light of political correctness and an invented racism, it perfectly works.

When OBAMA said "remake America" means "destroy America."

So OBAMA started a very serious operation now that this year is his last year of power when really hecan do all he want to destroy America as he planned long time ago!

So he started with many things!

What would be to continue to change the twenty-dollar bill?

A woman face will replace the face of Andrew Jackson, former American president!

But this is a huge shame or a crass lack of culture to deny the huge historical role played across seventeenth and eighteenth centuries by this great man Jackson in all American history, in financing, in war, in which who really fought as a president under the American constitution, in constructing many, many fundamental institutions that we use these days, and he was named a founding father of the United States.

Who has the audacity to denigrate and ignore such a valued historical personality?

Well, any other country will be more than happy and very proud to have such a huge American personality, where OBAMA and his men will step on it!

There is no serious reason to change any American bill, which represents no more than American history and pride.

And nobody thought to change the American bills with someone that whatever will be never would be able to promote to so high real value as Jackson.

I think that American Congress and Senate should debate this strange proposal and publicly to have something to say in this attempt of torturing the American history!

I have doubt that there are many political Americans today that can dare to think and rise to the such a high level as Andrew Jackson did!

But what OBAMA not to do such a thing like this? So OBAMA can do all he wants. Nobody will say anything.

Who would be the American white who would have the courage to oppose?

And who will be on this new American bill of twenty dollars?

Monastery in a leg? Guess the mushroom who is?

Well, 100 percent will be Rosa Park or Harriet Tubman or other black woman to make everybody happy.

The racism is a criminal terror as a huge fist in the mouth of any white. Racism invented by Liberals is so dangerous that whites gave up for long time to have the courage to mind you to not tell them something.

So that they approve everything.

The American Congress and Senate should be more present in American people's life, that what has happened now is a huge abuse of American democracy or is a very wrong interpretation of it.

Now the blacks will go beyond any imagination to humiliate and dominate the whites.

And OBAMA's occasional agitators fully work.

Recently they pushed a black Justin to go to Metropolitan American Museum of Art and sue them for exposing a masterpiece of Italian picture from the sixteenth century, *The Miracle of Loves and Fishes* by Jacopo Tintoretto.

Why are the blacks so upset on this masterpiece and ask with patriotic briskness to be put out in the garbage?

Because in this masterpiece, the Jesus face is painted in white!

Soon lots of huge demonstrations will be around the streets of museum.

And why did this famous Italian painter dare to paint the Jesus in his natural color white?

By the way, this famous painter lived in Italy and has no slightest idea about slave time that appeared from 1525 till the Civil War.

And hold tight, how many violent changes will be done in this OBAMA's last year of total power and a long process of changing name of streets, places, famous American personalities, buildings, pictures, in the Orthodox and Catholic Churches, bills, books, masterpieces, songs, and so forth, of destruction or annulment or repainting soon starting in order to satisfy the huge desire of revenge.

A process that never will finish soon because the history and civilization and traditions of America is more than hundreds of years.

In this sad and unnecessary and useless to America slave period, between three hundred and four hundred thousand Africans were brought as slaves from 1525 till the Civil War.

Europe has no slightest idea about these slaves and their hard life in America.

So the famous Italian Painter Jacopo Tintoretto could be convicted for racism.

Anyway, whites are finished, and any kind of opposition will not take place.

OBAMA even has a free hand to do everything he wants!

And so does Uncle!

Barak Hussein OBAMA was very clear in his presidential campaign in 2011 saying "I remake America". During 8 years OBAMA ruined America in all directions. So OBAMA became triumphantly a big cancer for America, an undesired accident OBAMA! Step by step American people understood that OBAMA acted like cyanide poison killing everything. Well known as dead hand every politician from Democrat party asked him strongly to stay away from endorsing them for something.

---

Jimmy would have kept talking for a week.

He was a doctor of talking.

We needed to go to classes fast.

We promised each other to meet again and continue the discussion.

Jimmy considered it to be interesting and relevant.

Bill said, "Don't think I'm an original thinker. It's not my creation. I shouldn't take credit for everything I told you! Everything is public, and anyone can learn about these real aspects of American society with its Liberals and Republicans. The press, television channels, radio, journalists, political commentators, editors, tens of books in libraries show everything and practically anyone can get this information. It's not a secret."

We ran to classes.

It was right on time.

# CHAPTER 14

# ERIC AND SURVEILLANCE

What?

Do I see right?

It seemed to be Eric. And suddenly I remembered Mr. Jack's order.

Now let's see what he was doing, where he was going, whom he was meeting.

I was excited.

I had never spied on anybody.

Hm!

I think I liked it.

Stupid Eric kept on walking without thinking for a moment that I was following him.

He was walking fast and glancing to his left all the time.

He stopped, waited, and then started walking again.

He did that several times.

I heard a short whistle, and Eric stopped and then started running back like crazy toward a car.

It was a Ford 80.

Somebody waved to him from inside the car.

He approached the car fast. He bowed ceremoniously, and a hulk of a black guy came out of the car and hugged him.

I couldn't hear what they were talking, but Eric said "Yes! Yes! Yes!" several times.

I could hear that because I managed to get closer behind him.

I don't think he could hear or see anything in those moments.

As far as I could tell, he was totally frightened.

He was so visibly intimidated by that guy like he was in front of God himself.

I was getting more and more curious, and I got closer a few steps behind him.

But he didn't have time to see me.

Damn.

The guy pulled him into the car.

It seemed to me that he forced him into the car because Eric tried to step back.

But the hulk simply kicked him in the ass, and it was done.

Eric simply plunged into the car!

He was theirs.

The car started with screeching tires, and Eric disappeared together with the car.

I had lost Eric. How could I find what he was doing?

Whom should I ask?

I shuddered!

What if the hulk wiped Eric out?

He was not my buddy, but he was black like me, and I thought I wanted to see him again.

Hm!

I was thinking that, and for some time I kept walking deep in thoughts.

And guess whom I saw?

Shit! It was Eric!

Sound and safe.

I was totally baffled.

Didn't they abduct him? Did they abandon him?

What the fuck was going on there?

I was dying to find out!

I started to follow him again closer.

He was walking calmly, and I could see something bulging in his back pocket.

I wondered what he could have there.

Well, I had to find out because Mr. Jack wanted to know.

Why only Mr. Jack?

I was even more curious.

The curious shape of the pocket looked like a gun barrel.

That was it! It was clearly a handgun.

And a big one too!

Real big.

I got scared.

What if Eric wanted to shoot me because I was following him?

He had no reason to, but you could always find something.

You know!

―⁂―

While following Eric, I passed Tom without seeing him.

That guy saw everything.

Where could you hide?

Tom said out loud, "What's up, boy? You can't see people anymore? Are you all screwed up? You're all screwed up so help me God! You know, your grandpa kicked the bucket and you don't even care? You're full of shit! Your grandpa wanted to make you a real man, but you always did what you wanted. I know everything. Don't lie to me, boy, 'cause I'm gonna smack your yapper! How come you didn't know?"

I tried to tell him I didn't know because I hadn't been home for the past couple of days.

Bullshit!

It was a lie, but I had to say something.

"You're such a fucking liar," said Tom. "You lie through your teeth all the time. I saw you with my own eyes yesterday when you were coming out of the house. I called out to you, but you didn't hear me, or you pretended not to? And you ran away. I couldn't see you anymore. Like somebody was out there to fuck you. You fucking moron. Your grandma was right when she said you're not gonna end well."

I replied, really scared, "What was I gonna do alone with my dead grandpa? As far as I know, it's something for the police or the hospital 'cause I got no money. I don't have a penny on me."

Tom yelled at me, "You asshole, it's not about the money here! I know you're poor as a church mouse and you're gonna be just like all these other guys. But seeing him for the last time, that's how you behave? How can you be so stupid?"

I mumbled something.

"Yeah, you're right. But I didn't know where the hospital is. You know, I'm in all kinds of trouble, and I'm a bit down."

"Go fuck yourself. You're a big asshole. Now that you're all by yourself, clean up and dress up and come see us at home. My wife wants to talk to you."

I was startled.

"Who, Michelle? I remember she was keeping me away so as not to corrupt her children, Drumm and Jenny. If she wants to talk to me, tell me when and I'll land there! I got plenty of time, thank God!"

# CHAPTER 15

## JEALOUS DICK

While I was washing and preparing to pay Tom a visit, I was talking to myself.

"I'll take my chances. I'll go there and that's it. I'll see what the trick is. There must be something to gain because that lady is always on the take. That Michelle could never stand me. She used to call me son of a whore. Honestly, she was right. My mom spewed me out and then took off. It makes me so sick to my stomach I don't wanna think about it. That is what it is.

"Enough with the self-pity. Fuck it. You know, Hillary is always ready for a fuck. Her pussy is on duty waiting for me."

But a stupid thought struck me.

"Do you really think Hillary is waiting for you? Is she counting on your cock only?"

"I got a cock as big as a cucumber. So what? Aren't there others like that?"

"There are guys with small cocks, and I even heard that guys with big cocks have big problems to get an erection. And they go to the doctors to give them fuck powder. Actually lots of them."

"But it's their problem. What do I care about their cocks?"

I looked in the mirror, and I was ready.

I decided the battle order.

First I fuck Hillary, and then I go to Tom.
Good!

---

In Hillary's house, there was a party of some sort.
The music was loud, you know, how we're used to.
Fuck the neighbors who complain about not being able to sleep.
I got into the house, and what did I see?
I felt I was going ballistic.
Hillary was almost naked and was making out with Rick.
I'd known Rick for a long time.
We had broken into houses and stolen together many times.
He was like a brother to me.
I couldn't count how many times we helped each other escape a police chase and hide stolen stuff in places only we knew.
Yeah! Only us.
Many.
I was speechless.
She saw me and said, "That's it. It's done. Go fuck Jasmin. She's got pussy too."
Up until then I thought Hillary loved me and no one else.
She told me once.
It's true, a long time ago.
I didn't like the dirty way she spoke.
It was not for a girl like her.
But everything gets more rotten by the day.
It was the first time my lover, or whatever you wanna call her, cheated on me.
It was a strange sensation, something real heavy pressing on my heart.
Well, Hillary was really my love.

It was only to her that I talked about special things and only her I told about Mr. Jack and the new life I had started to live under his harsh authority.

If I had a gun, I'd have wacked both of them.

It was not right that another guy fucks my lover.

I really couldn't share her with anyone.

It's different when you don't know.

But when you know, you're going nuts.

I knew that a lot of murders were done in our community.

Many times the police came and arrested another one.

What a dumb thing to be jealous?

Because that was it.

Jealousy!

I didn't know what the fuck I should do.

You feel alone forever and your heart is beating hard.

Your mind is out to lunch and you must decide what your next step should be.

Right now!

There is no thinking or reasoning.

What the fuck? The hell with it.

How easy for a girl to just say bye-bye!

No more pussy for you and that's it.

She couldn't understand or care all the pain and torment in her ex-boyfriend's heart.

How much pain and struggle to avoid doing some stupid thing.

How are you gonna live from now on without her pussy?

Lonely.

Real lonely!

Without her from now on?

That moment your mind is numb as if from jerking off too much.

You don't know anything anymore.

Have you completely forgotten how many other pussies are out there in the world?

How many you're gonna fuck, only if you look for them a little bit.

And even cooler than Hillary.

Shit.

---

The pain in my heart didn't go away completely, although I tried hard to reassure myself.

Holy shit!

I might croak because of so much pain and torment.

What a big sorrow came over me?

Where is this from?

I understood well why Larry wiped out those two.

He was jealous, and he couldn't take it anymore.

He was simply blinded by jealousy.

You can't think normally.

You're desperate, frightened, and you pull the trigger.

To unload yourself.

Why does the judge fail to understand how hard it is?

Grandpa probably laughs at me now.

There must be his hand into this, I'm sure.

Maybe yes!

Maybe not!

I was feeling miserable.

My girlfriend left me.

---

Many girls in our community had been murdered.

Mr. Jack told me many times he was going to see the judge to save some of our people from trouble.

It's right.

That's big trouble.

To be left without pussy and sent to jail just because you took a just revenge.

Do I know if it's just or not?

Who am I to kill Hillary?

She's got such a good, tight pussy, and she's so hot riding on my cock.

It was great to fuck her.

Too bad now.

But maybe there were other chicks like her.

Come to think of it, it was only pussy we're talking about.

Just like Larry said the other day, they're all the same.

Tried to calm down and go to Tom fast.

You know?

Tom was waiting for you.

Tom was home.

I knew he was a man of his word.

—⚏—

It was a nice and quiet afternoon.

Tom had got home a bit earlier.

He was waiting for me to have a talk.

I had just got into the house when Jenny, his daughter, came in sobbing and crying her eyes out.

Tom asked her, "What's wrong, girl? Some asshole tricked you? Or what the fuck is wrong with you? Tell me and then stop crying."

"He let me go."

"Who?"

"The manager of the special parcels department."
"You don't know him anyway."
And she ran to her room.
What room?
A shitty little closet you wouldn't call a room.
Small and low.
She threw herself on the concrete bed and started weeping alone.
No one could see her.
She was very heavyhearted.

Last Friday when she got into her boss's little office, he stood up and without saying anything grabbed her butt real hard and lifted her on his desk.

In the blink of an eye, he tore her panties off and started to tickle her asshole with his tiny dick.

At that point, Ping Kong, as she had nicknamed him, started to mumble something.

"Sit tight, bitch, it's not gonna take long."

In a few minutes, it was done, and a wave of thick oily cum started pouring from his golf-ball-sized balls.

That yellow cum dripped on his trousers and on the floor.

Suddenly scared, Ping Kong took a small napkin from his desk and wiped his trousers and the pool on the floor.

And he quickly shoved it into his pocket.

He tucked his little dick back into his pants and told her not to talk to anyone. Otherwise, she would be in big trouble.

"Boss! I swear I didn't tell anyone. I understood that it was a clear case of rape. But too complicated to go to justice. And for what? I don't even know if that guy fucked me or not? I really don't know. I for one didn't feel anything. Not to mention an orgasm. Nothing at all."

Ping Kong was huge black guy and so ugly you couldn't even imagine an uglier guy.

He was not married.

He lived alone.

Why?

When he felt something in his balls, he forcefully fucked some chick.

His arms were so strong he could play with anyone like a toy.

There were many women in his factory.

But rape was not the problem.

On Monday, when I went to work, I was called to human resources.

And the secretary gave me an envelope.

She didn't tell me anything.

I opened it up, and what did I see?

Ping Kong fired me.

I wanted to talk to him, but somebody said he had called in sick and would be back in a few weeks.

I called his cell phone but no answer.

Dead.

So there I was, fucked, fired, and penniless.

I was overwhelmed by tears.

Daddy called me to come to dinner.

I couldn't go. I was in too much sorrow.

Whom could I tell?

What a shitty life we women have!

I knew I was chubby. Even really fat.

When I looked around me, most girls were very fat.

I didn't get married, and I must live with a shitty family.

And suffer.

I thought of going away far from our black community.

A long time ago I even did it.

But I came back fast.

It was tough somewhere else for women like me.

And our men with their hard cocks had gonecompletely crazy.

They'd run after white girls and even marry them and move to other places far from here.

Shit.

They'd marry ugly white girls.

They might be fat or old, but what the fuck, they were white, and our boys want to whiten themselves.

If not them, at least their children.

And who's gonna fuck us? You tell me.

Lots of girls bought dildos.

I got one under my pillow.

It was always ready to fuck, but it was not like real black cock.

I swear, I was thinking of going to a damned doctor and have him sew my cunt closed.

Why should I suffer so much because nobody wanted to fuck me?

—⁂—

That motherfucker Ping Kong.

A big asshole.

He fucked me or he didn't fuck me.

At least he could have given me a few bucks tobuy myself some panties, stockings, or cosmetics.

Motherfucker.

Wait till I see Mr. Small Dick.

I'm gonna give it to him big time.

Mark my words.

I started to calm down a bit.

Later I went to dinner.

Well?

"So what?"

—∽—

There was that poor bastard Dick.
He was talking to my dad.
I don't know what they were talking about.
But I wasn't really interested.
It's all a big shit!
Later, even a bit too late, my mom came in.
She's a big Tramp.
I don't understand how come my dad, who knows everything, hasn't thrown her out yet.
I think his dong doesn't work well anymore.
Who the hell knows?
She had hardly got into the room, and without eating anything, she sat down near Dick started to scold him.
I know.
Dick is big moron.
He dropped out of high school. That honestly is a joke.
You don't have to do anything, just drop by from time to time.
For some of the tests, we're all cheating with the teachers' approval.
But he can graduate it whenever he wants.

# CHAPTER 16

## NEW DETAILS

The phone ring woke me up from my lazy rest.

I took the trouble to get out of bed and answered the call.

It was my pal Jimmy.

We arranged a meeting before lunch.

At the college campus.

I came on time.

Jimmy hadn't arrived yet, and I thought it was not nice of him.

He was not like that.

He had never made me wait for him.

Breathlessly he came running to me.

He said, "Hi, Bill. Sorry, old sport. Mea culpa. Let me tell you the reason. When I got into the building, the president saw me. He's a great man. He stopped me and invited me to his office. Inside there was this chick so beautiful my knees went soft. He introduced me. 'Mr. Carlson Jr. Ms. Lipinski Jennifer.'

"We skipped the 'Nice to me meet you' stuff, and Jennifer asked me, 'Do you know about the rape of the three students yesterday evening on the campus grounds?'

"I said, 'No! Absolutely nothing!'

"'Really? Nothing?' She stared at me and smiled.

"'That's all,' the rector politely said and left me clueless.

"What do think, isn't it something? I'm telling you, I'm coming from his office, and I'm a bit concerned. Honestly, I'd love to rape a stunning chick like that. But that's just dreaming.

## Dreams

Let me tell you the joke with the elephant in a bar.
"Tell me."
This Texan had a bar.
One day a Frenchman come into the bar.
He sees an elephant in the bar and asks the owner.
The Texan explained that anyone who can make his elephant laugh will get a thousand bucks.
Shortly after that, the elephant starts laughing out loud.
The Texan gives him a thousand bucks, and the Frenchman leaves.
Later, the Frenchman comes back.
He sees the elephant with a new announcement.
Who can make the elephant cry will get a thousand dollars.
Not long after that, the elephant starts crying and sobbing.
The Texan gives him the thousand dollars, and the Frenchman wants to leave.
Before he leaves, the Texan asks the Frenchman how he did it.
"It's simple," said the Frenchman.
"The first time, I told him my cock was longer than his. The second time, I showed it him!" says the Frenchman and leaves.
It's a good one. Really!
I was laughing like crazy.

---

"Now let's get to work," said Jimmy.
"We have a lot to discuss."

In his typical fast talk, Jimmy started to ask me if I understood the problem with the lying politics of the guy high up.

And if it was clear that racism in America is just a big fat lie.

Invented to scare the whites and to trick minorities, especially the blacks.

Because he didn't give a damn about the Latinos, the Chinese, or the Muslims.

When the racism problem started to became serious, I talked to many black and white Americans.

Nobody admitted that we have this problem.

Maybe in the sick minds of Al Sharpton, Eric Holder, di Blasio, and the big kahuna OBAMA.

I just happened to watch an interview with Trump.

What do you say? Have you heard about this guy?

I said, "No! Who is he?" I didn't watch TV.

"All are lying through their teeth just to get elected. The Republicans disappointed me the most. You got the power and you still do what OBAMA wants. It's too much. It's really just political fluff."

Time wasted!

Or maybe they are threatened with death somehow.

Who knows?

We're too small for this game.

I don't think we'll ever know the truth.

The white palace keeps us in the dark.

There are no real problems for American citizens.

You can see that every day.

But the high-up boss's gang must provoke agitation at all times.

How to fool the stupid masses.

Shit.

A baseball player admitted that he only fucks in the ass.

That he doesn't need any cunt of any color.

After hearing such a momentous piece of news, the horse, the high-up boss's wife, came out of the white palace and shouted happily, "Thank you for that!"

Several times.

I've never understood what the problem is with these guys who fuck asses.

I think it's a just personal problem.

In the end, it's a health problem.

I don't think Americans were interested in any way or had something to gain.

Talking about fags!

A hospital in London proved that ass fuckers are sick and that the English doctors had already saved many fagots by using electric shocks.

There is this recently saved fagot who was so happy he was cured that he founded the Homosexual Rehabilitation Hospital.

You know what they say, God spare us the moron's hard work.

But if OBAMA likes to get involved in everything, why not the horse?

That's how she started to instruct the students to eat all kinds of plant dishes that made the kids throw up and leave the school during lunch break in droves.

Did you see the reaction of students sick and tired of horse's culinary recipes?

They all come to school with their own lunch or buy at the store.

Well, yeah!

Now she is of aristocratic stock, you know?

When she went to Europe, she stopped directly at the king of Spain.

What do you think?

They all mocked her.

## THE DEATH PENALTY FOR KARL MARX

But she didn't care!

—w—

Let's talk about this Trump guy.

In the beginning, I was bored, and that's why I watched him.

A very rich guy.

Gradually, I understood that he worked real hard to make his fortune.

On an interview with the judge of the Fox News Channel, I was astounded to learn that he has never in his life drunk, smoked, or taken drugs.

Even more!

He raised all his children in God's faith with respect for any human being. They didn't drink, didn't smoke, and didn't take drugs ever.

Their education was very strict and serious.

Trump has never made any compromise.

All his children succeeded in their work through their own effort not through connections, gifts, or relations.

This man Trump has a clear and correct vision for America.

He doesn't want wars.

Quite the opposite, he wants to bring a lot of money into the country and build a true market economy and the foreign and domestic investors to compete to invest here.

Not in China or in Europe or somewhere else.

He is determined to make a strong America respected by the entire world.

Like any other country, he wants the world to know that you can't screw around with America.

He explained very clearly that right now we don't have a country and anyone from the outside comes here and does what they like.

He's right.

Millions of economic migrants have been secretly called by OBAMA who has already given a presidential order to legalize them overnight.

OBAMA knows exactly what he wants now.

Millions of votes will come out of blue sky.

Why did he call those poor people here?

For their votes!

Trump is getting infuriated by the many mistakes OBAMA made and keeps on making.

Trump had the guts to tell us the truth.

OBAMA intended to do anything in his power to weaken America.

Trump had the courage to say OBAMA is totally incompetent.

And there has never been such a weak, unqualified, and impotent president in the White House.

Shamelessly lying to the American people and dividing us at all times between blacks and whites.

Yes, OBAMA is certainly the most racist black in the world.

Probably it couldn't be better.

OBAMA is a poor president who up to an older age has never had a job, a guy who used to gobble drugs instead of going to school.

Maybe OBAMA wanted to do something good.

But life has demonstrated clearly that good intentions are not enough.

You also need brains.

And experience.

And seeing that he is closing in the final doom from shitty situation to shitty situation he started to be scared.

Hanging on to power at any cost is not only a burning desire but also the need to escape many responsibilities.

That way it's easy to create a frightened, terrorized America paralyzed by something that doesn't exist, but who cares.

The end justifies the means.

OBAMA desperately chose the racism card.

All the politicians have clearly said it!

I said, "I see no contradiction in everything you told me. It's very fascinating. I think and hope that Mr. Trump understood well the truth about OBAMA."

Again our discussion extended over a few hours.

We were excited and delighted that a true-born American, be it black or white, like Mr. Trump (from now on we are going to call him Mr. Trump only) managed to penetrate in a simple and clear way through the intentional chaos created by the Liberals.

Everything holds logically in Mr. Trump's speech.

All of a sudden we looked at each other as if struck by a revelation.

If the Liberals murdered Mr. Trump, then America is doomed.

We must be vigilant and watch everything OBAMA says and does, as well as his covert agitators under his direct command.

The fight has just begun against OBAMA, number one enemy of America for a real and just society for all.

Volunteers wanted.

Mr. Trump wants to make America strong again, so help him God.

I said, "Dear Jimmy, you're a natural politician. You see many complicated things so clearly that I'm astonished. With your permission, I'd like to share with you some of my recent research."

OBAMA was a child raised by his mother and grandparents in Hawaii when he arrived from Kenya.

I don't want to say more now.

When he got to Chicago, he was poor and penniless.

The state helped him go to school.

He lived for many years on welfare.

I'm sure there were times when he didn't eat anything.

A life without money, full of debts, and incapable of getting a job nourished his personal hate against all whites.

Even during the campaign, he declared he was not born with a silver spoon in his mouth like Mitt, his opponent.

An intelligent mind molded at the school of pain later threw him in the open arms of the Liberals.

Doing nothing else than the other Liberals were doing, he has never had any personal contribution in the Senate.

Nobody knew him, and nobody had heard of him.

He was a shy and obscure individual.

The feeling of racial inferiority, so visible in everything he does made him what he is today.

Now you know the story how he happened to be candidate for the White House.

A sort of curse for America.

You know that Carter was one of the weakest presidents before OBAMA.

OBAMA is the absolute champion in destroying America.

Carter is better known for the hostage crisis in Iran.

OBAMA lied with his "We don't leave our own behind" so that he could release many terrorists detained in Cuba.

Only lies with his health card.

He signs political treaties with and approves everything Iran does against America.

Even the new crisis with the hostage journalists in Iran demonstrates without any doubt that OBAMA is clearly the worst and most inadequate president for the interests of America.

The farce with the University of Washington, DC, is a laugh.

Nobody heard of him or his name as a student in that period of arduous studies.

## THE DEATH PENALTY FOR KARL MARX

The alumni of the University of Washington, DC, came on TV and declared that very clearly!

Maybe it's something with the University of Pennsylvania.

How can it be?

Was OBAMA totally invisible?

Too many lies can ruin everything.

Goodbye.

See you soon.

And we each went in different directions.

# CHAPTER 17

## THE RAPE

In the library, there were just a few students.

I saw her.

An angel from heavens.

And so beautiful like no other on earth.

Bo, a Korean girl from Seoul.

A body to die for.

And the eyes!

Oh my god, the eyes.

Large and dark and displayed on her face in a most fascinating way.

Something that will disturb and hurt your heart at the same time.

Something designed to kill any man.

Even the girls felt a bit disturbed in her presence.

I said to myself, "It's not fair! It isn't! Her seduction force brings too much drama. I swear, she is a permanent crime against us men all over the world."

I remembered a story of a very sexy girl, Fedra, who was murdered by her husband's father because of the much suffering that her fascinating beauty provoked.

But I think Bo was much more fascinating and charming.

She inspired a crazy, unstoppable, and incomprehensible passion.

She seemed to simply penetrate through your eyes directly into your soul.

She just got there without asking you or getting your accord.

She didn't ask anything.

She was just there in your mind and your soul, and anything you tried to do to escape her superb image was useless.

She was like that.

I don't know if she knew or cared about the dramas she created in us the people around her.

I was following her with my eyes all the time.

I was more determined than ever.

This evening it's got to happen.

This evening must be my evening.

Gazing at her, I didn't realize that Joshua and Willis were right behind me.

I remembered about the plan.

I must work.

No matter the risk.

Yes! No matter the risk.

---

Bo stood up and headed to the library door.

I knew every single move she made.

I'd been following her for over seven months.

And I knew her schedule by heart.

Now she was heading to the department parking lot to meet her boyfriend.

A very lucky guy, I swear.

Very young and handsome.

Green eyes, light complexion, and deep-dark hair.

Tall and I would say perfect for Bo.

But the horrible jealousy in my heart wouldn't let me admit the truth!

Ah! I would wipe them all out.

One day maybe.

The guy worked in the Secret Service.

Big kahuna.

---

I started to perspire.

I was watching her very intensely.

The two guys were behind me.

I could feel their breath.

They were too under a great stress.

The plan was clear. We couldn't forget any detail.

Bo walked down the stairs, stopped for a second, and started again without seeing us.

I was perspiring profusely, and a funny feeling came over me.

I said out loud.

Must be done and that's it.

I couldn't take it anymore!

I couldn't!

I looked back. Joshua and Willis were following me, and we signaled with our eyes.

When Bo came near the flower beds in the department alley, I ran to her like in a daze and took her hand.

Very quietly, she said, "What do you want, Jeri?"

I forcefully took her in my arms and tried to lay her down.

With and unexpected strength for such a delicate girl, Bo turned to me fast and slapped me hard on the cheek.

She banged my head with her bag full of books, and I staggered.

I called the guys for help.

When Willis grabbed her arm, Bo shoved her knee hard into his groin, and he fell down groaning like a dying animal.

I couldn't give up.

She couldn't be stronger than me.

I punched her hard on the right ear.

Bo swayed on her feet.

Curiously, she didn't scream for help at all.

My punched had dazed her, and she crumbled slowly to the ground.

I pulled down her panties and started to have sex with her.

I was another man, liberated.

Not a man tormented by her charms for over a year.

Now she was mine, and maybe she'd stay with me.

Who knows?

I came.

It was unbelievable.

Bo hadn't regained consciousness yet.

I quickly pushed Joshua on top of her.

He took out his cock, but it was so soft he wanted to give up.

He started to jerk off and got it hard.

He was pumping her hard.

Bo wasn't moving at all.

She was still out and limp as a cloth.

I looked at Willis.

He was still moaning because of the pain in his balls.

I pushed him too on top of Bo.

He started pumping, and in a few minutes, he was done.

Suddenly, I got terribly frightened.

I realized what we had done.

I viciously beat Bo so we could fuck her against her will.

That was rape!

We ran away like desperate animals chased by death.

—⚏—

There was nobody home.
I lived with my mother only.
My father had left when I was two years old.
I hadn't seen him too much after that.
I was a strong, well-built guy bulging with muscles.
More so since I'd started body building.
Everything was perfect except the head.
My dick was even bigger than Joshua's.
I knew it well because we had measured them several times when we were in the shower at the gym.
How about the head!
Well, that was a real joke.
Ugly joke.
Imagine a body over 1.90 meters tall and a small head like a five-year-old child's head.
I was tall, and I felt miserable.
Totally unhappy and in pain.
I know that I looked exactly like my mom.
I understood why dad had left her.
Each time I met a girl, she was visibly embarrassed and wanted to leave fast, invoking all kinds of excuses.
But I was crazily in love with Bo.
"Oh, God, why did you bring her into my life?"
I'd never hoped that Bo would be my girlfriend.
She was much too high for me.
I knew it.
And it is not easy.
I met Bo on the varsity stadium some time ago.

# THE DEATH PENALTY FOR KARL MARX

We were training for football, and she used to run on the track around the field.

She always wore long sweatpants, although if you saw her legs, it was a delight.

She was very serious in everything she did.

Her father was a dentist in Korea, and he went to China after the divorce.

Very quickly he got himself a new Chinese wife, really good-looking and thirty years younger.

Bo knew she wanted to do with her life.

She lived in her own world.

It was impossible to get inside there.

Only the lucky ones.

Certainly not me!

---

Joshua had another story.

He was an honest, ambitious black man.

He wanted to get into the police force or something like that and have a career.

He had recently come from Alabama and enrolled in the college program.

He was always busy with women.

I think the white girls were riding him a bit too much.

Although his complexion was so dark, it could scare you at first sight. You liked him when you got to know him.

He didn't have too many ideas, but they were fine.

He was not interested in politics.

He didn't know who the vice president was.

And when it was about the revolution, he used to say grudgingly, "This OBAMA guy deluded my poor people."

I suddenly remembered Willis.

He was a nice boy with no spine.

He was incapable of any initiative.

Although he was handsome, he was not going after chicks.

It was the chicks who directed him.

Otherwise, he wasn't interested in them.

Willis was the kind of man who needed a boss to tell him what to do.

Anything!

But a boss.

I couldn't understand why he was so shy, but one day he told me.

"My mom used to beat the crap out of me. For absolutely no reason. She has never loved me. Although she was alone with me in the house, she didn't care what I was doing. I was probably the freest child in the world. A lonely child deprived of motherly love because she was very disappointed by her former boyfriend with whom she had me sit in front of the TV and she used to weep at her favorite soap operas. She didn't tell me too much about my dad."

I stood up to get something to drink from the fridge.

I felt a terrible shiver grip my heart.

It was real.

I raped Bo, and I wasn't happy at all.

Quite the opposite, I felt bitter and scared.

More so than before.

Now I loved Bo even more, and I deeply regretted what I'd done to her.

Why didn't Joshua and Willis stop me?

They even encouraged me.

I had no expectations from Willis.

But Joshua seemed to be smarter.

I was a fool.

An idiot.

A big moron.
But it was no use. Everything was lost.
And Bo was like an angel.
How could I hurt her so much?
The poor thing, she fell down like a leaf.
Why didn't the fool cry for help?
Maybe we would have gotten scared and run away.
It would have been just an attempt to rape.
Now we were deep in shit.
I deserved everything.
I think I'd go to the police.
I knew that girls are not strong, but she was amazing.
I started crying in desperation.
It was getting harder and harder.
I used to hate myself for this ugly head of mine, but now the pain was killing me.
Stronger and stronger.
Unbearable.
Later on my mom came home.
She switched on the light.
I didn't realize I was sitting in the dark all this time.
Mom asked me, "What's wrong with you? You seem distressed. Can I talk to you later? I'm going to take a shower first."
I said to my self out loud, "You're a horrible beast. What am I going to tell mom? That I hit Bo so hard she almost died? That I raped her? Like a criminal? That I pushed Joshua and Willis to rape her as she lay there like dead?"

I went out into the street.
I was hoping maybe Bo didn't go to the police.
Maybe she was ashamed.
I knew she was very proud.

A wave of joy swept over me.
Maybe.
I swore I would never ever do anything that dirty again in my life if I get away now.
Thinking about it, it wasn't even sex.
Something in a hurry and very scared.
I solemnly promised myself not to do it again.
There was a church on my street.
A big and beautiful one.
I didn't know if I ever got into it.
I went in.
I prayed for hours with more passion than ever.
I was feeling better.
Now I was in God's hands.
I really didn't care anymore.
He would decide my fate.
God help me.
Thank you, God.

# CHAPTER 18

## IN JAIL

A young cop said to us shortly but without any hate, "Get dressed out. Here. Now."

I didn't understand and kept my underwear on.

So did Joshua and Willis.

The cop said again, "Take everything off!"

He examined us attentively and told us to bend over in front of him.

And he clearly asked us to spread our butt cheeks and asshole.

We did it.

We did it.

He gave us some orange uniforms, exactly our sizes, and escorted us to the cell.

All three together.

The interrogation started.

Simple but prolonged over days and nights.

Always the same questions, and they always asked us to sign some papers.

We were never threatened or frightened somehow.

Very professional.

The food was good, even good quality.

We had thought we would be starving from then on.

Not at all!
And the police officers were very friendly.
But they didn't talk to us.
Only during interrogation.
That's it!

Time was passing slowly.
It was deliberate to let you think about what you have done.
The schedule had to be followed to the letter.
Nothing was allowed or possible outside the schedule.
Waking up very early in the morning.
Short time for washing.
Food in the cell.
A short time outdoors so you don't miss it too much.
Lunch in the cell.
And that's about it.
In the beginning, it was difficult to shit and pee in front of others!
It was so embarrassing!
Where was my bathroom, my toilet, my cleanliness?
Slowly I became an animal.
I couldn't see anyone and wasn't interested in anything.
I had begun to understand that I deserved everything for what I'd done.
I was determined to die.
I don't know how, but I was thinking all the time.
Sexual life, zero.
Sometimes I would jerk off in the bed at night.
Joshua had become very intimate with Willis.
That was not my business.

Suddenly another convict made an unexpected gesture.
And very clear!

Cut your throat.
He conveyed to us the message we were in big trouble.
All pussy rapists must pay a special price in jail.
It was the unwritten law of jail.
Day after day and mercilessly!
There was no escaping from it.
You get beaten to death or worse.

I was gone anyway.
First by my self-hate.
I even wanted to be punished by the other convicts.
I fully deserved it.
During that long, long time, I thought of what I'd done a million times.
I behaved like an animal.
I knew it, and I didn't ask for mercy.
No punishment was enough for my vile behavior.
Gang bang!

One day I was told my mom came to see me.
The policemen said, "It's you in a female version."
I understood the hint.
I looked exactly like my mother.
Mom was older and uglier.
She tried to comfort me.
I was nervous, and I left before the policeman came to escort me.

Willis got a simple advice from his mother, "Don't bother to come back home. There is no place for you anymore."

Completely abandoned, he was living his life drama in full.
His mother had never loved him anyway.
That's why he was so gentle, soft, and without personality.

He was suspiciously indifferent.
He executed everything anyone told him like a robot.
That's why he ended up in prison.

Joshua's case was different.
His father forbade him to come and see him.
He was in grief.
And sad.
How could Joshua do something like that?
He was ashamed in front of his friends, coworkers, and himself.
He couldn't accept that he had raised an animal, really a criminal.
He decided not to see Joshua ever again.

That moment made Joshua weep and suffer a lot.
He didn't eat anything for a week. He refused to go outdoors and didn't speak to anybody.
Days later he started to feel a little better.
Bit by bit.
But the grief never disappeared from his heart.
One day I looked carefully at all the other convicts.
They were all cheerful and ate and worked out in the gym all day long.
They were in the mood for action.
I was horrified.
I understood.
After years and years of prison, you don't care about anything and anybody anymore.
You are not yourself.
You are a faded image of what you used to be.
Prison turns you into an animal, and the slightest feeling of pride, desire, or hope is dead.

Now when I needed to shit or pee, the shame and privacy and self-respect had disappeared.

And we were not yet in the real jail.

We were not convicted yet.

The trial was still far away.

They were gathering evidence, hearing witnesses, putting together a jury, and so on.

I didn't need to discuss with anybody.

About what?

All we talked about was the rape and nothing else.

Why?

Why?

And I couldn't find any excuse!

# CHAPTER 19

## TRIAL TIME

After a long period of time and a lot of suffering, we were announced that soon we would go to trial.

I don't know why the police needed so much time for the investigation, declarations, and more declarations.

It was all so simple.

I participated in a gang rape'

But I think everything is designed to make you suffer more, regret, and wish you would die.

Or maybe to make you immune to any court verdict.

There were a lot of people in the court.

I think those people are sadistic.

Or something.

The police had us dressed in a suit and tie.

It was worse for us.

I felt like howling in pain and my heart was shattered.

Cops at every door.

The judge was a young and beautiful woman.

Tons of evidence, declarations, reports to confirm such a simple fact.

Rape!

It was a unique moment when Bo who looked like a dream pointed to identify us.

She knew us very well.

From the college.

Many witnesses I had never seen before, a lot of people in the jury.

The trial was intentionally long-winded, and I was watching the jury.

A fifty-year-old white man who was fretting like he had hemorrhoids.

Three blacks a man and two women, one so fat you expected her to blow up.

And five white women of different ages.

I suddenly asked myself if these people are entitled to punish me.

I was looking around to see a familiar face.

I don't know why, but that's how people are.

We don't know what we want.

Maybe that's why I was there.

I remembered lots of things about the rape.

I had studied it sometime in the past.

I remembered that in ancient times, women were considered like an object for men's pleasure.

If a woman was raped, nobody cared.

Even in France's Louis XIV, the parliament voted to hang rapists.

But for the next fifty years one, two or three were punished.

I started to be convinced that our rape must be mediated by authorities.

To have some kind of deal.

So that anything can be solved with money.

That way both the victim and the culprit win.

The government gets rid of being responsible for the culprit and the victim starts a normal life.

If you put the culprit in jail, nobody wins anything.

Quite the opposite, you have to feed them regularly.

For free and for many years.

That's why maybe we had a chance to go home and go back to college and reintegrate society.

But what if the jury really wants us to go to jail at all costs?

They don't care about us.

I think they are very bored and discontent even if the court pays for their work day.

A rape obligatorily requires a trial.

Being accused of a crime is a desperate and hard-to-bear situation.

You have to know what right you may still have under law and to immediately act to defend yourself.

A rape is an illegal sex act against the will of the other party.

The essential element if forced vagina penetration without consent.

Women suffer an enormous psychological trauma when the aggressor is not punished for her rape.

Before the seventies, many courts saw force as one element in the judgment.

The lack of consent is the necessary element in any rape.

A woman suffers tremendous psychological pain and humiliation when she has to go to police and report the rape.

She is then sent to the hospital and waits a long time to be examined and for evidence to be gathered in order to sentence the rapist.

She must tell the story of the rape several times and to repeat those moments that are very traumatic for her.

For that reason, only 16 percent of rapes are ever reported to the police every year.

The lawmakers understood what a heavy burden is for a woman to report the rape.

They created the USANE program that facilitates the procedure of reporting a rape.

Another serious problem in any rape is if the victim defends herself during the rape.

If the victim defends herself, it may become much more dangerous for her.

Many other things came to my mind during the trial.

If I really think about it, it's not even our fault.
It's nature's fault!
Sure.
What did it create such a beautiful and delicate being as Bo?
What did it endow her with such much power of seduction?
You feel you're going nuts!
Your mind stands still and you think how you can reach her?
You forget about the law, morals, responsibility!
I used to be a very honest law abiding man!
Now I'm waiting to go back to hell.
For what?
For gang rape!
My head is spinning.
I didn't understand anything anymore.
Is there any solution for sad, uncomforted lives?
God is great.
I desperately prayed him to forgive our sins.
Religion always says to confess and God shall forgive all your sins.
I became more optimist.
Maybe there was a good solution.

The judge stood up.
Everybody was anxiously waiting.
What's it going to be?
What was the jury's verdict?

That moment my life and my friends' lives depended on those jurors.

Good God help us!

The judge received a paper from the jury.

She stood up.

And everyone else in the court room.

"Guilty."

My life had just been erased from the face of this earth.

Twenty years in prison with no chance for parole!

I couldn't feel the strong hands that led us back to where we had come from, to jail.

We went back to hell.

# CHAPTER 20

## JANE MARRIES

Jasmin was putting some makeup in the mirror before going to work.

She was secretary to some bone doctor.

She was twenty-nine years old.

She was very attractive, and many boys and men were sincerely longing for her.

She had a simple principle.

And would do anything to abide by it.

"As much sex as possible every day."

Some time ago on a Saturday, she had had crazy sex with Jeri, a student with not much money but a lot of dick.

The next day she brought home with her Willis, a guy so shy and respectful that she took pity and gave him a good fuck.

After thirty minutes of sex, she remembered that Joshua, a well-hung black guy, was supposed to come over.

She asked Willis to finish fast, wash, and get dressed and be on his way as soon as possible because she had just remembered her mother was coming to visit her.

Willis didn't finish but got out of bed and went to the bathroom to wash.

She heard some weird noise, and when she opened the bathroom door, he was jerking off just to let her alone.

She had never seen anything like that, and thank God she had had a lot of fuck partners.

When Joshua came over, she told him what happened to a good friend of hers.

That Joshua guy was good to fuck but not to go out with him.

He was poor, almost penniless, a frigging student.

Joshua spent like two hours and then left.

Guess who came to visit her later?

A lady friend.

Jane was very reserved and didn't like to talk much.

But she came to tell her what had happened to her at work the last couple of days.

She was having a chat with a girlfriend waiting for the time to go home.

The secretary called her to give some information to a customer.

It was a tall, nice-looking black man.

They were introduced, and unexpected the black invited her to dinner the next day.

She went, and that was that.

Ray, the black guy, charmed her immediately and told her he would like to see her again and introduce her to his mother.

She met his mother, who was a big, fat, and very friendly black woman.

She kept wiping the sweat on her face, neck, and hands every two minutes.

They discussed about many things.

Ray told her shortly he wanted to marry her.

And he asked her to marry him.

The engagement ring was ready, as if everything had been prepared in advance.

The ring was a bit loose, but it can be fixed at the jeweler store.

I was stunned and tried to say it was too soon and...

Ray didn't let me finish, took me in his arms, and fucked me till I passed out.

What could I do?

I didn't try to resist, and honestly I wanted a good fuck.

I was dizzy with the fuck, and I accepted.

I said to myself, "If he keeps fucking me like that, I'm the luckiest girl on earth."

Later I found out he was supposed to marry a black girl in the neighborhood.

All preparations had been made.

And whether you like it or not, people eventually find out everything.

Sanga was a girl who had come from Ghana two years ago and now she was pregnant with Ray's child.

What a shitty situation.

I don't know what to say?

Sanga told me everything straightforward.

She had been sponsored by a white American guy for nineteen years, and two years ago she immigrated from Ghana.

She was very dark, and it was really difficult for a black girl to get married as the few unmarried black guys are crazy about white girls.

Ever since OBAMA came to power, more and more black guys wanted to marry white girls regardless if they are old, ugly, fat, or have white kids.

The guys with money, though marry the super hot white girls.

Look at Kardashian or Woods and many others.

They want to whiten, if not themselves at least their kids.

The lack of black men is a bid and difficult problem for black women.

Many don't get married and blame the white girls for stealing their men.

I remembered Dannay, a good friend who had been married to a black guy for many years.

She was not happy but had lots of sex and she thought that in life it was good to have a guy to pumped you good and hard. There was nothing else.

Everything in life was his holy cock. Who cares about religion, education, respect?

She wanted to get a divorce many times, but she didn't decide yet.

She told me that her former white boyfriends who fucked her like crazy didn't even want to look at her now.

Even her mother was sad and avoided to bring her two grandchildren in her house in Mineola.

So that's how it is.

When a black man marries a white girl, the black women suffer and put a curse of her for stealing their man.

In certain cases, they really kill them.

I was shocked and couldn't say anything.

I remembered the story of a black guy from Nigeria, Muhamed Hosein Barhdan, who wanted illegally get into Great Britain.

"If I get to Great Britain, everything is solved. "Many white, fat, and ugly women will marry me fast, and after three years I get my documents and divorce them as fast. And then it's my time to choose a white girl I like.

"I can see them from here how they are waiting for me and will be all over me. You have to be a smart guy because women are eager. Nothing about respect or love or a common future."

He went on:

"If you got a good-sized but lively cock, you're a made man. Not all, but most women need a good fuck, not religion, education, respect, love, or color. If their mother and father are disappointed and don't agree? No problem. The holy cock is number one almost everywhere around the world.

"It is true that in some countries, there is respect for parents. But not in America, Canada, Western Europe."

How to solve such a tough problem?

Sanga was a twenty-one-year-old nice and sexy black girl.

At first glance, it was a difficult situation, but slowly I remembered the world around us.

She was not the only girl who got pregnant before marriage.

She could even ensure a good future being a single mother.

The American culture is simple: you make one or two kids and don't ever have to work.

The state will provide everything you need.

The young black guy, Brawn, from Ferguson, was not even twenty when he got shot by a policeman, and he already had two kids with two different women in the hood.

He had no job and no income to raise them.

Or the case with the thirty-year-old black man who had no income and had thirty-one children with seventeen different women.

And the state took care of all his children.

The state even wanted to castrate him to stop him from doing all the damage.

Oh, forget it.

Well!

I thought there was no problem for her to marry Ray.

If she felt good impaled on his cock, that's the important thing in life.

Nothing else!

Morals are for idiots.

The holy cock is the most important thing in the world.

So Sanga may as well fuck another guy and feel good.

Why should she regret being abandoned by Ray?

She was not the first and certainly not the last case.

I said out loud and seriously, "Don't even think to refuse Ray. Do you feel good in his cock? Hump his hard and that's all that matters."

Jane enjoyed my advice very much and took out her cell phone to call Ray and tell him yes.

After chatting a few minutes, she told me she felt better, and she was quite happy.

She couldn't believe how fast got she rid of morals, religion, and her European culture!

Sex is number one!

Very young virgin girls under sixteen are running after men who don't deserve them and bring so much suffering to their parents who can't understand that and can't accept the shame.

For good sex!

We talked for a while longer, and then Jane left happy and reassured.

She would marry Ray soon.

At the office a fifty-year-old woman came in. She was very sick with arthritis in the shoulders and knees.

She was in great pain.

I talked friendly to her, and we finally got to talk about sex.

She told me I was so young and what a pity was to miss a chance to have sex.

She said that life is short and men are chasing you until you're forty-five.

After that, they start to avoid you.

She went to see the doctor for treatment.

I received a call from Jane, who enthusiastically invited me to the restaurant.

Ray wanted to meet my friends.

I went out dressed to kill.

I sat down on Ray's left side, and we started to chat and eat dinner.

After a while, I felt a leg who was rubbing against my leg insistently.

I quickly withdrew my leg and was astonished.

What was Jane going to say about that?

I would never tell her.

She's my best friend.

"I swear!"

I thought that maybe it was a mistake and everything was going to be fine.

But Ray kept rubbing against my leg, and I was getting embarrassed.

Suddenly an idea struck me.

Why not?

I shouldn't refuse even the slightest chance of a good fuck.

So what if she's my best friend?

She would never find out.

And I didn't withdraw my leg.

Ray understood he won.

He flashed me a big smile and went to the washroom.

I went quickly after him and gave him my phone number.

That was all.

In less than a minute, I had a new cock at my discretion.

We talked about life and work, and then I stood up and went home.

Even before I got home, Ray had called me three times.

He had even left me messages.

I was a bit surprised it was too soon, but that kind of stuff happens.

I gave him my address, and in no time he was knocking at my door.

I didn't ask anything about Jane.

What could I ask?

I had something else to do and fast.

However, I asked him if he really wanted to marry Jane. He said yes.

On the table there was a newspaper with the picture of some faggots, two young and handsome boys.

I asked what he thought about that.

He said, "It's our luck because there are fewer of us looking for pussy."

He told me he thought those guys are clearly sick and need medical treatment.

He went on, "What I don't understand is why the government is so interested in encouraging them, protect them, and exacerbate their disease. Let them be. They like ass, let them look for ass. Those guys have serious health problems. Poor schmucks. The government shouldn't even take them into account. Some have AIDS and others have purulent boils in their assholes and yell in pain when they have to sit down. Why should we make parades for them and encourage them in other ways?"

The other day, Lady Boss in the White House came out and shouted, "Thank you for being a homosexual!"

Three times.

Why?

Or the young baseball player who publicly declared that from now on he wanted asses and nothing else.

These things shouldn't be made public.

Not at all.

When the Supreme Court decided to allow them to marry one another, the big boss OBAMA who is a gay as many people said put up special lights on the White House.

From white to pink.

In my opinion, the Supreme Court should make decisions on serious matters of those that have an impact on society, like the Senate and the Congress.

The vote should be valid only starting at minimum 67 percent, something like 6 to 3.

That 5 to 4 is inconclusive.

Never a simple majority.

But maybe there are other interests, and I don't get it.

Ray was as chatty as a woman.

We parted with the promise that Jane would not find out anything about it.

A few days later, I got a phone call from Jane, who said she was happy for getting such a good fuck from Ray and that she made the right decision.

I called Jeri, an old-time friend, but he didn't answer.

I left a few messages, but he didn't call back.

I tried to talk to Willis and Joshua.

Not a chance to talk to them.

I gave up, but something seemed funny.

How come I couldn't find any of them?

Maybe I'd find them another time.

I was just thinking how great it was to be a good-looking, sexy girl for whom all the guys are drooling and hoping to fuck one day.

Only a few percent of girls are ravishing and drive all men crazy.

The many others struggle the best they can to find a place under the sun.

They have another more realistic and correct philosophy.

But the few percentage smashing girls have special philosophy and a special life.

We know that you can do whatever you please with any man.

They are crazy about your pussy.

Just a little sign, a wink, a simple smile, or a long glance, and he is yours.

They become submissive, kind, respectful, happy, flatterers, generous, impressionable, attentive, easy to maneuver and exploit, soft, aroused, charmed, seduced, ready to do what you ask, crazy, terminated.

They wouldn't refuse you anything.

They'd sell their soul to get some money to fuck you.

They'll pay for restaurants, luxury items, anything you want because they desperately hope that soon they'll get to your pussy.

They'll do whatever it takes.

But there's something funny here.

They are crazy about your sex, but they'll never marry you.

They marry other girls, but they are crazy to have sex with you.

I was laughing with a girlfriend of mine about what Leonardo da Vinci said about sex.

His sex tormented him his entire life, and it was so stubborn that you do only what it dictated you to do, and whether you like it or not to must obey it without questioning.

When morals, responsibility, respect, religion, and fear of God disappear, that is all you have left.

Sex becomes number one in your life, and you are no longer interested in anything else.

But there is clear and present danger.

Sexually transmitted diseases.

If you don't trust your stud, you ask him to wear a condom.

It's not like before, but it's safer.

Therefore, there are no limitations and no reasons to quit.

Some women addicted to sex declared on TV. They adore sex even if you can get AIDS.

So what?

Sex is more important than health.

I read somewhere that in the Trobriand Islands, some primitives found out there is a disease with no cure, we call it AIDS, and in the end, you die, but it's still good to have sex and everybody needs it.

Civilized or primitive, the world is the same.

Sex comes before anything else.

After many great fucks, I unexpectedly met Jane.

She was mad at me and wanted to avoid me.

She told she had nothing to say to me anymore.

That I was a hopeless whore who would do anything for cock.

I told her straightforward, "Just like you, darling."

Holy cock.

Cock in everything and before everything.

We didn't talk much, but she told me she wasno longer with Ray, that he was crazy about pussy, and that she had had enough going for all kinds of treatments for STD that Ray brought home.

And then she added with a sigh, "I think it must be the black girls' curse because I stole their men."

One of my girlfriends who was in the same situation told me that the crazy sex with Derly didn't last long.

For over a year, he had started to complain about pains in his cock, and the doctor told me to get some tests.

He's got a huge prostate, and several times he couldn't pee, and in the hospital they gave him a bag with a catheter to help him pee.

I think I'd separate pretty soon.

At least it was good I didn't have any children with him.

I got married to him because he fucked me good, but now he's like dead for me.

I guess those poor black girls who couldn't get married and live alone because of us put a curse on us white girls.

God punishes every sin.

It was pleasant, warm summer evening.

I was having dinner with my new boyfriend.

He was a very intelligent guy who was graduating soon.

A few big companies were already competing to hire him.

Jimmy knew a lot of jokes and liked to tell them bluntly.

He asked if I wanted to hear one.

I said go ahead.

Because I had just come from a good fuck, I was relaxed and in a good mood.

Jimmy started.

It was silence in the classroom, and all the students were listening to the lady teacher.

Outside it was gorgeous May day with clear blue skies and singing birds.

Only one student was looking out the window and sighing.

And so on.

The teacher saw Baldy and asked him what was wrong with him.

Was he sick or something?

The student said he was very sick and didn't know what to do.

He was a hermaphrodite, and he knew his life was meaningless and he wanted to die.

The teacher soothed him and promised she would take him to the school doctor.

In the medical office, the lady doctor started to examine him and saw his long fat cock and told him he was not a hermaphrodite.

Quite the opposite, he had a great dick that many girls would be desperately eager to fuck him.

Baldy then said with a sigh, "Doctor, you tell me I'm healthy and I got a huge cock. That I'm not a hermaphrodite and I should relax. But I know I'm a hermaphrodite!"

The lady doctor was puzzled!

"I got this huge cock, but you see my head, it's full of pussy."

I laughed my head off.
Great joke.

After a while I saw a guy who looked like Willis.
I tell Jery how much he looked like a friend of mine, Willis.
He was startled, and he asked me, "You know Willis?"
Yeah, and let me tell you, I'd never met a more shy, well-mannered, and softer guy.

Well, he and two other guys raped a very hot girl and each received a twenty-year jail sentence.

Now I understood why nobody had been answering my calls for over four months.

Jimmy wanted to pay the bill, but I knew he was a student and didn't have too much money.

I paid the bill. I was surprised to learn about Willis and went home.

Jimmy wanted to have sex, but I didn't invite him to my home.
Another time, for sure!

# CHAPTER 21

# DICK, JOHNNY GREEN LEE, AND ERIC

"Life is good," said Dick, lounging at a table on the patio and busily munching on a McDonald's sandwich.

He thought, *There's not too much to do.*

He was thinking of what Michelle, Tom's wife, had told him.

Was he going to be good or not?

"I'll see later. I'd don't feel like thinking about that right now. Anyway, the house is on Grandpa's name. The motherfucker died a bit too late. He lived poor as a church mouse anyway. It was nice he got the Social Security check that saved him every month."

---

Lookee, lookee! Hold on tight! Look who's getting into McDonald's?

That's Johnny Green Lee.

He looks good and seemed to be cheerful.

I met the guy once when he came to Grandpa and chatted until late at night.

And he asked for a few bucks because he was moving to Queens.

He swore on his life he would pay him back the money soon, in a month or two.

I swear, not a day later.

Yeah, right!

He never paid back the money.

He vanished.

As if the earth had swallowed him.

I know from Grandpa he was complaining what a scumbag that Johnny Green Lee was and he was sorry he had swindled him so easily.

I got no idea how much money it was.

I said, "Hey, Johnny Green Lee, what're you do in' in the hood?"

He looked at me.

He asked me, "Who the hell are you? Eh! Have we met before?" And he started to go away.

He glanced at me in a funny way and headed to line up and grab something to eat.

I said, "I met you at my grandpa's! He used to live on Forest and… You know, he kicked the bucket the other day."

"Who's that?"

"Oh!"

He vaguely remembered my grandpa.

"What was wrong with him?"

"I don't know."

I replied, "Cause it was his time."

Right?

Johnny Green Lee smiled and said, "Are you gonna eat a sandwich or are you done?"

I thought it wouldn't be bad to chow down a bigger sandwich.

I said, "Why not? Bring it on to Papa."

I wouldn't leave the place for the life of me.

We talked a lot.

I had all the time.

I had just turned twenty-one.

I was in my prime!

Suddenly I asked him, "Why did you come here? Are gonna stay and live here? Or is just for fun? To fuck some fresh cunt? You can count on me. I got tons of cunts. Good and cheap. Come on, don't be shy!"

He said, "Well, I'm married now with three kids and one more on the way!"

"Okay, forget it."

"I came here to stay somewhere for some time. I don't know for how long."

"Why? Are rents so high in Queens?"

He said, "That's no problem because Social Services don't let you hang there. They help you. If you got kids, you don't even need to work. Why do you think all the broads make kids and wait for the Social Security envelope? Not too shabby. They don't even know who the father of their little rats is. White and black broads do the same.

"Long live the pussy. That's your American culture working. And they all learn the trick very soon! You know?"

A bit embarrassed, he continued, "To tell you the truth, it's my fault. I was always making scandals in the house, and the people on the lower floor kept filing complains. They used to bang the ceiling with a broomstick to make us stop. They used to shout, exasperated, 'Stop making so much noise. For God's sake, we are people too, and we need some quiet to get a few hours of sleep at night.'

"I don't know why, but it made me real pleasure to make noise and get onto those guys' nerves. With no job to do all day long, you kinda get bored. The family under us were two poor retired people. He used to work in construction, and she used to be a social worker, the kind that go house to house to ask people all kinds of questions. They didn't have any children.

"I would bang a piece of wood from morning to evening, then I would run around the apartment with the two kids, but the best effect was pushing the table and chairs on the floor around the room. They made an awesome noise. We would make a real cool noise in the evening when all out family we used to jump on the floor till it buckled."

I asked, "Even your wife used to jump up and down?"

"Sure thing. We are a united family. What do you think? The apartment building was old and the floor squeaked real bad. But we discovered portions of floor that drive you crazy with squeaking. Me and the kids would play on those portions for hours, and the squeaking was indescribable. But it was all legal. It wasn't our fault. The building was at fault.

"When I left home, I used to put a power tool with the motor on directly on the floor, and it was making so much noise you felt like banging your head to the walls. We were not home, and nobody could say anything. Later I found out that flushing the toilet was a good source of noise. Sometimes at night I used to let the shower flow full blast.

"You know, those guys' bedroom was right near the bathroom, and nobody could get any sleep anymore, guaranteed! We would stop for a couple of minutes and then start again and so on.

"Another surefire source for scaring people is to go downstairs to the intercom panel and ring somebody to open the door! That noise wakes you up from deep sleep and scares the shit outa you. The lower floor neighbors woke up tens of time a night and asked who it was. An hour later we would go down again and drive them nuts.

"Some other time we would sneak in front of their apartment and rang the bell till they went ballistic. But it didn't work for long because the schmucks switched off the bell and the intercom connection. Then we used the phone, and in the middle of the night, it's really cool to get phone calls. But they switched that one too one night.

"That's why we're left with the old sources of noise. Until the super comes over and tells us to stop. It's hard with so many in a one-bedroom apartment."

"How come they gave you only one-bedroom for the entire tribe?"

"We lied and said we were freshly married. It's easy if you mumble something about racism. OBAMA's racism is the fashion now. It works like a charm. You whisper it, and everything is solved. Yeah, a smart guy, this OBAMA!

"On the floor above us, there was this young Jew with a hot wife. He had two kids and his mother-in-law. They only made a little noise when they walked around. But at night they were quiet so that me and my family could sleep. But during the day there was noise. The rest is okay. They had installed some thick carpets to attenuate the noise. We were bored, and that's why we made so much noise, you know?

"But that's not it. I don't why, but me and kids we used to pee and shit in the elevator many times. The super got it fast. Motherfucker. In the beginning it was easy. I barked out at him, 'What? You have the guts to offend me? Why, because I'm black, right? If you don't cut the crap, I'm gonna call the police right now. You'll be in deep shit for bothering an innocent man.'

"The super shut up and went back to his office. A few months I didn't see him, not even in the building. All was good. After a while, he formally invited me to his office. There was also a woman and a fat Jew from the management. He politely invited me to sit down. And then with short gesture he put some photos in front of me.

"When I looked at them, whom do I see? Me with my cock hanging out and pissing all over the elevator walls. Another picture with one of my kids shitting on the elevator floor. And not just one photo. Some of them were very crisp. Real crisp! What could I say? The racisms scam no longer worked!

"I stood up to apologize. The Jew says, 'You have a letter here. In two months you are leaving this building. And then he was gone.'

Only the super was left. I tried to apologize to beg him to let us stay, promising I won't pee in the elevator. Zilch. 'Go somewhere else. I am small here.' They said, 'You must go and you better do it quietly. Otherwise they'll evict you forcefully.'

"Pissed I got caught, I said, 'It's okay, OBAMA will help me!' I'm still thinking. Mendez, the Mexican super, was fucking smart, the motherfucker. Tough asshole! Look what he did to me? He installed surveillance cameras in the elevator. That's how he nailed me.

"No problem he saw my cock, but he saw me pissing all over the elevator. My wife told me, 'Why do you pee in the elevator? It stinks real bad. It's not like you don't have a toilet. Hold it until you go up. Now that they're throwing us out, it's no big deal, but who the hell's gonna accept us now with an asshole like you?'

"That's why I'm here. I gotta settle somewhere with my whole tribe, don't I? But not for long. I'm already missing the life on 199th Street in Kew Gardens near the Metropolitan. I'll see how it works."

Johnny Green Lee went to line up for a bite to eat.

It was long line, you know, like at McDonald's.

Later, he came over with the food.

He dropped it on the table and said, "Gobble it up all. Don't leave a crumble."

As I was sitting down and munching, who do I see walking by? Guess who?

It was the cocksucker, scumbag Eric.

I didn't know what to do.

I asked him, "Bro, can I go out and talk to a good friend?"

He said, "Beat it! Go on, run. I'm gonna finish my chow and I'll take off too. Bye."

I replied, "See you."

Outside there was nobody.
Eric had vanished in thin air.
No trace of that asshole.
I looked around me.
I couldn't believe it.
Eric was coming toward me.
He was not really my friend.
He said, "Nigger, did you see your mother?"
But he stopped.
He didn't say what he usually said, "Give her a fuck from me."
It was better.
For both of us.
Eric whispered, "Can you help me? Now's the time!"
And he dashed away like crazy.
I went quickly after him.
What's up with this wacko all of a sudden?
He didn't really say anything.
I don't know.
But I gotta find out what the deal was.
Mr. Jack would be proud of me.

Eric smelled like drugs.
Sure.
Of course!
I knew how drugs smelled.
I'd taken so many my self.
I even had a few on me.
But Eric didn't care about me.
He went straight to a short, fat Mexican with abig moustache, and without saying anything, he put his hand in the back pocket.
He took out a big handgun and killed the Mexican.
On the spot.

Nobody had time to react.
The Mexican was lying dead on the sidewalk.
Real dead.
Blood everywhere, no kidding.
I saw stuff like that in the movies.
Only in the movies.
I'd heard about that kinda stuff, but when you see them in front of you, it scares the shit out of you.
My heart was beating hard as if I had shot the pocket-size Mexican.
I was speechless.
"What? Why? How?"
There was just a blur in my head.
Eric didn't say anything.
I was scared and couldn't understand anything.
Maybe Eric was going to say something.
But Eric jumped in a car nearby and took off with screeching tires.
I saw clearly.
It was a Ford 80.

# CHAPTER 22

# MR. JASON

Jimmy came looking for me.

He was breathless, and he said shortly, "I can't sleep at night. I got to tell you. You know that black guy Mr. Jason from finance and administration? He told me something you won't believe. I asked people about racism. Black and white. I even asked Joshua.

"By the way. The idiot is in the slammer. I don't think we're going to see him for the next hundred years, maybe in another life."

"What did the bonehead do?"

"He took part to a gang rape of a beautiful student. He had so many other chicks. Why did he need one more? It's true Bo is more than a dream, happiness just to touch her. So what? He had it coming."

---

I'd known Mr. Jason for some time.

He was almost a friend.

He was very smart.

He'd been working in the financial department for two to three years.

Yesterday I saw him on the corridor and asked him, "What's up with this racism that's driving America crazy?"

He looked at me. He glanced at his watch and said, "Do you have some time?

"Plenty" I replied.

He invited me into his office.

"Sit down. And be quiet. Do you still work at the department magazine?"

"Yes," I said.

---

And he started talking.

"Jimmy, I'll tell you straightforward! There is no racism."

"Not at all?"

The other evening, I was talking to a good friend of mine.

He was bitter.

I'm so ashamed in front of people with this racism!

But where is racism?

You can see that I'm black.

Nobody has ever forbidden me to do anything.

I got a house in a white neighborhood.

My wife is white, and she is great in all worldly things!

My kids are going to a good school.

I can ask for a loan at any bank at any time.

I can go into any store and buy whatever I want.

I can dress the way I like.

When I'm not driving my hot, new car, if I'm riding the subway, a bus, or an airplane, nobody bothers me.

OBAMA has completely flipped out.

Same thing here at work.

Everybody is doing his or her job and minding their own business.

I am really ashamed about the way OBAMA keeps pushing this racism stuff.

It's all his creation.
You know that he's an American Muslim.
He's not an African American.
May be that's why he hates whites so much.
Even his grandparents used to have slaves in Hawaii.
That's what I heard.
I don't know for sure.
My friends are just like myself.
They don't see and don't feel an ounce of racism.
And they are ashamed too.
A good friend of mine, Clay, told me that millions of blacks like me feel really embarrassed.
We simply feel ashamed in front of the people around us.
In front of all the honest white people.
When all the doors are open to you to study, to create, to do business, where is the racism?
It's true that it's all up to you.
I feel like howling with shame.
I'd like to become invisible sometimes.
The trouble is that none of the blacks in top positions do anything about this bullshit.
On the contrary, they stir it up to stink even more.
I feel so embarrassed and angry that I'd like to go to OBAMA and tell him to shut the fuck up and stop perpetuating this hoax.
Great, great shame on us with this made-up racism.

Stupefied by what I'd just heard, I said in a low voice, "But how about all those riots almost every day? Hordes and hordes of black people in the street, creating a pandemonium, breaking into stores and stealing and none of the higher-up bosses stopping them, quite the contrary, pushing them not to give up!

"They make sure that the mob has plenty of freedom to loot and break in, and ask the police to step aside and try to fend off the stones and bottles hurled at them. Do you know what happened in Baltimore?" I asked again.

Mr. Jason almost snapped at me. "Sure, I know. But that's another story. It's too long and I don't have too much time."

But he couldn't go away and added, "Millions of black people like me have built a good life for themselves. OBAMA's racism thing is a big humiliation to us. It's like asking for mercy and begging for help.

"It's the expression of stark helplessness and a clear proof that a black man can't succeed by working hard and abiding by the law. Without education, seriousness, respect, hard work, and discipline, nobody has ever succeeded in this world. "Life is not easy for anybody. I liked very much what that genius of a guy Bill O'Reilly from Fox said. That's it. You need education and a united family. OBAMA's racism is barefaced begging.

"We ask the whites to forgive us for not working, murdering, fucking without restraints, and taking drugs. I enjoy when I see black husbands and wives. Nowadays, less and less.

You end up like this by doing nothing but dancing, stuffing yourself with all kinds of drugs, avoiding school, and making children all over the place without any responsibility or care. There is no more respect for the law. They are the police clients. And the police is hindering them a bit. So death to police!

"They fight for more money and privileges form OBAMA. Nobody asks for education, jobs, respect of the law. Noooooo! Just death to police! The streets are wide. There's plenty of room for a lot of people. Why did OBAMA and his gang start this determined Total War Against Police?"

Only police was still able to stop them from their main activities like selling drugs, gang turf wars, or raping.

They wanted to be left alone.

If you look closely, it's mostly young people.
It's a pity.
Such a pity.
Nobody asked for education, jobs, respect of the law?
Why?
Well, they don't need any of that.
They live a pretty good life without too much effort.
A lot of money comes from Social Security.
If you make a couple kids, you're in business.
The good life.
They have housing.
Cars, TVs, phones, and everything they want.
And they need to scare off the whites.
Because you know it's racism.
Let taxpayers pay for it.
Why? Because they have the money.
The Liberals have been there for over a hundred years.
That's all they could come up with.
Even OBAMA told them during the Baltimore riots.
The Republicans are to blame.
They cut some money of the billions that I generously gave the blacks in Baltimore.
And the rioters all shouted, "Death to police!"
And they are right.
OBAMA knows he used them to get the top position.
He knows he can't give them anything.
So you got to stir up hard the flame of hatred and racism.
You shouldn't let it die!
Against the police and always against the whites.
I'm sick and tired of OBAMA's lies.
All the people who take part in all those riots are always the same guys.

The get paid for it.
Agitators take care of them!
And he said out loud, "Shame on him!"
Racism doesn't exist, but OBAMA needs racism badly.
Liberals don't want to risk losing power.
Power is sweet and advantageous.
You know?
Over 60 percent of the blacks live like me.
Therefore, racism is a hoax.

Mr. Jason sighed.
"Could you come see me in two days?"
"In two days?" I asked.
Mr. Jason continued, "I really feel relieved. Telling about OBAMA's racism, I feel relieved of lies and shame."
I went out of his office.
I couldn't get over my emotions.
I said to myself, "Gold! What Mr. Jason said is pure gold. I've never thought like that."
I was convinced that all the black people were kneeling in front of the big boss when it came to racism.
How could it be that 60 percent of black people live and think like Mr. Jason?
Gold! No joking.
I was overwhelmed by emotions.
I had to see Bill right away.
He'd be shocked! Just like me!

## CHAPTER 23

# BILL KNOWS A LOT

Jimmy looked for Bill for some great news.

I called Bill and we met the next at the university.

I was very agitated.

I felt I was going to blow up.

I needed to talk to somebody.

I was choking with excitement.

How come 60 percent of black people didn't believe in racism?

How come 60 percent of black people haven't heard or felt OBAMA's racism?

I blurted all out.

Bill said, "Now you see how things really are? Truth comes out eventually. You know, lies have a short lifespan. So the tale that the policemen are racist and intentionally kill black people is a big scam. Listen, you don't really find out what happened and don't respect justice, you can invent anything you want?"

Just remember the big noise around Ferguson.

The cop was right.

He was defended himself against Brawn, who was high on drugs and was walking in the middle of the road.

When the cop told him to go to the sidewalk, he got really pissed off.

How could that piece of shit cop tell him what to do?
And he lunged toward the cop to teach him a lesson.
With his fists because he was big and strong.
It was not good, and honestly I'm sorry he died like that.
He was young and inexperienced.
He was a victim of the racism hoax.
After that, OBAMA started denigrating the police, like Al Sharpton, you know, indoctrination, and the Holder, the big racist, followed fast by di Blasio.
"Don't stop me! Don't shoot!"
And symbolically raising your hands is another story.
The fact that it soon proved to be a shameless lie that caught the entire America doesn't matter.
The boys tried to trick us.
It didn't work! So what?
They've got other lies ready to spread.

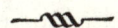

---

They know well.
The police will do its duty.
For them you're not white or black.
You don't screw around with the law.
Everybody knows it.
I liked that black sheriff Clarky when he said on TV, "Do what you're told to do. It's for your own good."

As a police officer, you're sometimes faced with an imminent social danger, and you have to do something to restore law and order.
Faced with a determined army ready to fire or with a covert one but also ready to fight, the policeman doesn't have too much time to think.
He can only shout, "Put down your gun! Put down your gun!"

He's got only one life just like you.

I suddenly remembered my father.
He was a cop.
He died in the street like a dog.
Fatally shot!
And then slashed up with a knife to prevent identification!
Maybe he was afraid of OBAMA's racism and he didn't shoot those black guys who shot him without thinking and without mercy.
Those poor young guys were high on drugs and had no intention to comply with the Police order.
They were wasted.
Dead men.
They were going to jail anyway.
But dad wanted to spare their lived at any cost.
His kindness cost him his life.
Now we know that the Racism problem is not black problem.
It's a false problem spread by OBAMA, Eric Holder, Al Sharpton, and Mayor di Blasio.
They have on their hands the blood of all the innocent policemen shot with no mercy.
I totally agree that no cop should kill a defenseless innocent person whether black or any other color!
No! That's not good at all.
But they are far from doing that.
I'm pretty sure that every day before going out there on patrol, they are thoroughly trained to think a million times before using the gun.
Only in an extremely, absolutely dire situation.
The New York chief of police declared he wanted to hire more black policemen, but he shyly admitted he could find candidates because most black men have a criminal record.

# THE DEATH PENALTY FOR KARL MARX

I was surprised.

So that's it.

OBAMA lied again with that tale there are more blacks in jail than in school!

And as usual, it's the white people's fault!

I think the chief of police was shy saying that to avoid being accused of racism by Del Lazio.

This new mayor is a big racist without a reason.

And he started to screw up big time, even with that hole in the budget.

When he took over, the city had millions of dollars in surplus.

The city is now full with piles of garbage

What can you say about the Subway Stations?

On rails all kind of newspapers, magazine, cans, bottles and all kind of things and over these piles of garbage lots of rats with their new kids playing and running.

I think it is normal to penalize the ones that mess or to ask the millions without job which received only lots of money just to vote, to clean the rails that are so disgusting and unpleasant when day after day the piles are bigger and larger and smellier.

It is true some places are clean.

These people take in exchange money for doing anything.

Give them some work for the interest of the city!

And many places in city with piles of garbage.

They smell to kill anyone!

It is a huge and permanent unpleasant situation to see tons of garbage in any subway stations with thousands of rats and their new generations.

But you have to know the mayor is very busy with other special problems!

I suspect that it was with his implicit accord that the black man from another state came to New York and simply killed in broad daylight two police officers who were quietly eating their lunch in the patrol car.

I suspect the Liberals of having approved the crime.

It's clear.

The black man came straight to their car and *Bam, bam!* Done!

It was planned long time ahead!

It was mafia-style assassination.

The black guy than calmly tried to disappear inthe subway.

When he was caught by the people, he acted as programmed.

He shot himself.

I have no doubt about it.

I don't remember ever hearing about a black guy shooting himself.

I really haven't heard it until now.

It's like a terrorist job, like ISIS or al-Qaeda or something.

Do you think policemen are fools?

When di Blasio came to the funeral of the two killed cops, all police officers turned their back to him and booed him.

That protest was against all of them, Eric Holder, Al Sharpton, di Blasio, and of course, the biggest Liberal boss.

---

Slowly but surely the Liberals are losing voter trust.

They are desperate.

They know they can't win the elections in an honest fashion.

OBAMA destroyed everything.

Economy, NASA, insurance, army, police, constitution, immigration, health, school, and foreign and internal affairs.

He doesn't need public schools.

Sure thing!

His daughters go to private schools only.

Public school is not for them.

Everything he touches is finished.

It's like he's contagious!

Before the elections, all the Liberals avoided him like the pox.

This smart-ass senator from the South was going around with OBAMA and his family's portrait like some kind of holy relics to convince the voters.

She lost big time.

The people are sick and tired of him.

The biggest liar in the history of the American presidents.

That's what he succeeded in the White House in over seven years.

Remember what he said about the Medicare made to order?

If you like the doctor you had, you can always keep him. If you like the Medicare you had before, you can keep it, and he kept lying on and on.

Remember what that poor, slow-witted Nancy Pelosi used to say out loud in the Senate.

"You don't need to know what's in OBAMA's big Medicare file! First vote for it and then you'll find out!"

And the docile Liberals vote for it.

And then it was done, OBAMA has slammed us with another big pile of shit!

How about the crime in Benghazi!

OBAMA and Hillary had nothing to do with that allegedly.

They were completely innocent.

Well, you know, as a president, everything good is all due to you.

But when a whole bunch of screw ups come out, something must be clear!

It's not his fault!

Others are guilty.
He didn't know, didn't see. He's squeaky clean.
He's allowed to preside high up there.
Nobody is supposed to bother him with nonsense.

---

But OBAMA continued to lie about Benghazi for days.
A few weeks later during the UN session, he repeated the same lie.
He had no shame!
I had just come back from university when I heard that four Americans were killed in Benghazi.
I was very surprised and I wanted to find out more.
OBAMA and Hillary appeared on TV and declared clearly, "An American Muslim writer published a book about Islam that angered and agitated the Libyan Muslims who unexpectedly started a riotin Benghazi. Four Americans from the US embassy in Libya fell down victim to this spontaneous riot."

---

I was extremely affected.
How can you oppose a spontaneous riot in Benghazi and how can you save the four Americans from the US embassy, Ambassador Steven and three soldiers?
I believed absolutely everything that OBAMA said.
A month later, the same explanation at the UN in front of representatives of countries around the globe.
And there was no chance to save the American citizens in that embassy.
Slowly, life went on.

But suddenly I heard on TV, radio, and other legitimate news sources that OBAMA had lied again.

How many times has he done it already?

No!

There was no spontaneous riot in Benghazi.

It was a clear terrorist act where a few terrorists were involved.

More than that, it had been planned long time before to coincide with the September 11 anniversary!

Same date as September 11, 2001!

What's even more sinister is that the four members of the US embassy had desperately asked the American government for help long before the terrorist attack, about two months before, requesting more defense personnel.

Therefore, OBAMA lied shamelessly.

A lie I can no longer accept.

I used to believe in OBAMA's honor and gave him all the credits.

And OBAMA lied to me through his teeth.

I have the guts to only talk in my name and must say that OBAMA humiliated me, totally disregarded me, and ignore me.

I used to show my respect to him as our president. But today I've lost all respect or consideration for him.

An American president must respect his citizens and not humiliate them or treat them like fools incapable of understanding the real problems of our nation.

Lie is a very heavy burden for a just and honest person like me.

But why shouldn't he accuse the others?

And I repeated furiously, he was fast to accuse a poor writer for writing or making a film about the dangers of Islam.

He had no shame declaring, "The spontaneous riot of thousands of offended Muslims leads to their death. Three soldiers and the American Ambassador, Steve a notorious faggot."

And the lied worked.

Even if the world knows now that those poor bastards had been asking OBAMA for help and protection two months before the attack.

Nobody cared about them.

I won't accept that.

I am an honest young American, and I love truth and peace and respect for truth.

Everybody knows now that OBAMA lied incredibly. But he never ever apologized for this miserable attitude toward American People.

What to understand?

And why?

That clearly means that OBAMA does not care about the truth.

He already got systematically lots of Pinocchio trophies for his lots of lies

But no shame! For him everything is all right!

I found out that many people like me change the TV channel when he started talking!

Is this really good for a president? He lost his voice forever!

---

Now OBAMA is very concerned to protect the Muslim at any price.

More desperately now, after the new terrorist attack in California.

This attack is normal with his permanent policy to protect the Muslim in the world.

Just to pretend that they are peaceful people is ridiculous. They never like us.

Just fancy you are killed on the street because they are Muslim. For what? And why?

By what right OBAMA convicted me to real chances to death?

And all the time he makes fun about American People, allegedly they are coward and scare about Muslim kids and women. Ha ha ha!

Well, kids Muslim killed lots of American and swore to destroyed America.

Remember in France the criminal who killed lots of people were Frenchmen.

We can say all Muslim. But to be killed you need only one. Who is that one?

So you do not try to protect us?

By contrary, you permanently try to have from me my unique chance to protect myself! You try to interdict me to defend me and my lovers taking my gun from me!

You have to know that you are very protected by Special Forces because of the protocol!

Me, I am alone in front of your very peaceful Muslim!

The late remorse or regrets are time-consuming. It is pure and simple fluttering

---

Capito?

So that he can stay in the White House and play golf better and better and live the good life.

The position of US president automatically offers a lot of privileges.

Therefore, you must take full advantage of them!

He didn't care a bit about the truth. Most of his subordinates do the same.

The lie and lie and commit all kinds of abuses and illegalities.

And keep on lying.

Congress is like a doormat.

The create all kinds of commissions that don't solve anything.

What can I say!

It's just make believe.
He can't do anything!

The Liberals understand they have no more chance.
But they try all kinds of stuff.
Ted Kennedy is probably down there in hell because he can't be in heavens after all the stupid things he's done.
He can't get them out of the shit where OBAMA got them with his patriotic socialist revolutionary enthusiasm!
I'm pretty sure he would approve anything even a coup d'état just to stay in power.
Less and less Liberals still believe in him. Others know it's all a lie but don't care.
It's not easy to lose a lot of money, power, respect, advantages of all kind!
Its' time to save their skin.

———

Now there's a new hurricane raging over them.
Mr. Trump.
This guy indeed believes in opinion polls and the hope for real change.
He's got 30 percent in some states and going strong.
Why not?
He's honest, is against corruption, wants to cut taxes for regular people and raise them for the rich, develop the economy, gives a job to anyone who wants to work, and makes America big again.
Isn't it great?
OBAMA kept repeating, "Yes, we can!"
What can we?
Shit on America?

Turn America, the dream of every man on earth, into a Socialist Cuba?

Enough!

Mr. Trump opened our eyes.

He's got everything.

Billions.

Women.

Everything.

He wants the presidency so he can stop total destruction brought on by OBAMA.

No other candidate, except Craz, had the guts to publicly tell the truth.

The fact that OBAMA is a dangerous president for America.

That he's not interested in the welfare of regular Americans.

That he will remain in history as the weakest American president.

For everything he says with unprecedented courage, Americans appreciate him and hope to see him in the White House.

They will al vote for him.

A few dedicated Liberals have already pledged they will vote for Trump.

He can speak fluently, logically, and on the subject for hours and that is something that Americans haven't seen yet.

OBAMA even with his teleprompter stutters.

Mr. Trump wrote books.

And he knows business by heart.

He came just in time.

Now.

God protect him from Liberals and their evil ways.

Now we have to do something to help him.

America stands one chance only.

# CHAPTER 24

## JENNY IS ON TO PING KONG

It was hot.

    She was sweating profusely.
    It looked like the year before hadn't been that hot.
    She was walking to the bus stop when she saw him.
    Oh!
    I'm gonna kill him!
    He's gonna get it from me now.
    How long have I waited for this moment.
    Like a vulture she plunged to devour him.
    It was Ping Kong.
    In person.
    When he saw her, he tried to hide.
    No chance.
    He was mine.
    Full of anger, Jenny shouted real loud, "What a small world! How about that? Why did you fuck me like that? And why did you fire me? Eh! You behaved like a criminal. Answer me or I'll kill you!"
    Scared, Ping Kong invited her to get a coffee.
    They sat down at the table.

# THE DEATH PENALTY FOR KARL MARX

Ping Kong started to shake.

"What can I say?"

Poor me.

He asked me, "Did you go to the police? I am really sorry. I don't know what got into me. I'm so ashamed I could die. I am old and very sick. I got heart problems, walking problems, problems with my bones, and I take a handful of pills to be able to drag my feet. I'm half-dead."

And very scared he asked me a few more times, "Did you go to the police?"

And he was all shaking like a leaf.

Strange.

That mountain of hate in my heart melted away in a second.

I understood that Ping Kong was as good as dead.

Just like he said.

He was just a mountain of a man on the outside but deep down just a pile of shit.

And a very soft one too!

Finished forever.

I almost felt pity for him.

A bit embarrassed, I said, "And that's why you fucked me?"

Is this a man?

He's just a mummy.

He was cringed in fear and pain.

He was hardly breathing.

He choked a few times while drinking his coffee.

Suddenly he took out thirty-seven dollars and twenty-five cents from his pocket.

He held it out to me and said, "Take it. It's allI got on me. When I get some, I'll give you more."

And he started coughing badly like he was about to die.

Foe a few minutes I couldn't speak to him.

An unexpected pity crept into my heart.
This guy was a helpless bastard.
I was dreaming of revenge, lots of money.
Shit.
This guy was more miserable than I am.
That's my hard luck.
Fucking bad luck.
I asked if he wanted to go.
What could I do?
I felt pity for him and for me.
I stood up and waited for Ping Kong to do the same.
You know what?
The guy was immobilized by a lower back pain.
A spasm of pain contorted his face.

I walked out alone, and I was thinking of that woman who woke up one night with a black guy by her side who had broken into house and wanted to rape her.

The girl told him to his face, "Only if you put this condom on! That's the only way!"

In court, the judge rejected her complaint, saying that was not rape.

That she didn't try to defend herself and gave him a condom.
I was thinking of her and of me.
At least she was raped safely.
She was certainly fucked.
But me, nothing.
Because that mummy Ping Kong didn't do anything.
Fucking idiot.

With the shitty money he gave me, I bought a pair of panties and stockings.

I thought I should keep in touch with that jackass and scare him with the police because he's such a chicken.

Two days later I called him.

He was home.

I thought that I didn't have anyone and I might as well pay him a visit.

Ping Kong had a nice house with a lot of flowers a freshly painted in blue.

I knocked on the door.

He saw me and opened the door.

Now we were good friends.

He was alone and I was alone.

He told me to sit down and went to get some juice.

It took him a while because I thought he had died.

I didn't find any juice, and so I made mint tea.

That's all I got.

But it's healthy.

Drink that until I come back from the corner store of those Muslims.

He didn't ask me if wanted something or what I liked.

Ping Kong doesn't care about me and has no respect although I'm a woman.

He couldn't care less about me!

Twenty minutes later, he showed up with some bags.

He bought some salami and garlic bread.

He liked that.

He ate almost everything.

He didn't ask me anything.

That guy had forgotten I was there.

What manners.

I said to my self, "He's got no money, no manners, not even a good cock. You know, a good piece of meat to make a woman feel something inside. What am I gonna do with this jackass?"

But I thought he must have some money somewhere.

In the bank or under the mattress.

Some girls at work told me he had been working in that department for thirty-one years.

I took a look around the house.

This old fart thought I was stupid.

There were two rooms in the house.

In the first one there was the bed.

It was dirty and it stank, so I got out fast.

In the other room, there was a wardrobe and some living-room furniture.

I opened up the door wide.

There was some change in plastic bags.

Too heavy to take out.

I curiously peaked behind them.

I saw a cardboard box.

I tried to open it.

There were just one and five dollar banknotes.

But lots of them.

I reckoned it was my right to stuff them in my purse.

I filled my rather small purse, and when I was about to get out of the room, the old fart said to me, "You bitch, don't be an asshole. This money is for my funeral. You're gonna leave me penniless."

I told him I wasn't putting it back no matter what.

He started crying and sobbing.

And he kneeled before me.

I hit him with my purse, and I rushed to the door.

Did you think Ping Kong was a fool?

In front of the door, there was big crate, and the door seemed locked.

I was a bit scared.

Should I fight this poor bastard? Should call for help, or should I look for another exit?

I dashed at him and screamed out loud to scare him off, "You gonna go to jail if you don't let me go home!"

Quietly as if nothing had happened, Ping Kong took a big kitchen knife and headed toward me.

I was in danger.

What do I hear?

Somebody was knocking at the door.

It was loud and startled me.

The door opened wide, and another giant like Ping Kong got in.

He asked, "You limp dick, are you home or not? What the fuck are you doing? Did you forget? It's almost four o'clock, and we gotta go visit Mike in the hospital!"

He understood the situation right away and said, "You're such a stupid motherfucker. You gonna get in deep shit again. You've been missing jail life? Give me that knife and let's talk."

I took advantage of this lucky break and flew out of the house.

The shitty old fart tried to run after me and stop me, but he couldn't keep up.

With my purse full of cash, I stopped at the first store.

It was a men's store, not for me.

But I was calm.

There were people around.

---

I got into my room.

Nobody saw me.

I counted the money.

There was a lot.

At the bottom of the purse, I found several fifty-dollar bills.

About eight hundred seventy-four bucks.

I was so glad.

Now I had some money.
The old fart had something to give me.
I had something on him.
I was smart not believing he was poor.
A few days later, all the money was spent, and I called Ping Kong.
He was in bed claiming he had a liver problem.
He was excruciating pain.
I told him I was coming to him to talk business.
I threatened him that if he tried to do anything foolish, I was going to call the police.
He promised.

No change in the house.
Just like before.
I went in and said out loud so he could hear me.
My dad knew everything, and he might come here any minute.
He understood he must work with me.
From now on, he was under my protection.
If he didn't fuck me, wait and see how I was gonna fuck him.
Fuck till you drop.

# CHAPTER 25

## THE REPAIR SHOP

The car repair shop was located near some furniture stores.

The boss was a Polish guy called Ronsky, a mean fellow who was very good with cars.

He knew any type of car inside and out.

Everybody went to him when they had a car problem.

First he would caress them saying *"Rien Rien,"* but he told them immediately what needed to be done.

We appreciated him although we were a bit afraid of him.

The Polack could kick you out in no time.

If your work was good, you were his man.

Tom's son was a mechanic's assistant there.

You know, the guy who holds the toolbox and sometimes takes the car out for a test drive.

Drumm was his name, and he was respectful and appreciated by everyone.

Only the Ronsky used to call him Dumb.

He didn't mind and did his job quietly.

He sometimes followed Benny, a very handsome black guy who enjoyed much success with the ladies.

Five years ago I heard him talking on the phone with his wife.

He couldn't talk more politely if he was speaking to the queen of England.

"My queen."

"My dream."

"My jewel."

"My treasure."

"My love."

"Sweetheart."

"Tell me what you want me to do."

I was speechless.

My god, he was a smooth talker.

He was always smooth, enchanted, and horny.

Two days ago, Fredi, a German mechanic, installed some spark plugs and worked on the ignition system.

Short time later, the client hurried back to Ronsky's.

Something was missing from the car trunk.

He called Fredi and told him sharply, "Get out now. Go to the office to terminate your contract. I don't wanna see you again."

Fredi responded calmly and sure of himself.

"I want to know for what reason."

"Here. Now."

The client was angry and complained that a Japanese camera was taken from the trunk.

Fredi said, "I don't know anything about that. I've never opened the car trunk. It wasn't necessary."

Everyone was curious.

Nobody worked anymore.

The boss screamed at him and threatened he was going to call the police.

Very angry, Fredi left the workshop and headed to the office of the boss.

That was when Benny stepped up and said out loud, "I don't like injustice. Can't stand it."

He talked to the angry boss and whispered something in his ear.

That's how a black man saved a white man from big trouble.

And they were not even friends.

The German couldn't stand Benny.

Stealing is real bad.

You lose everything on the spot.

The boss called out to Fredi.

"Fredi, stay. Come over here. Go back to work. I'm really sorry. But you know how it is at work. People make mistakes."

Fredi turned to the boss and said, "Thank God. I really don't understand anymore. I'm going out to have a smoke."

And he walked by us with sad figure that looked like it wasn't him anymore.

He was an honest man, and being accused out of the blue for something you didn't do is really a big personal drama.

I was delighted.

I didn't know almost anything about Benny.

Benny was not only a good husband but also had a big heart.

And brave.

Days had passed, and the incident was forgotten.

I heard Benny talking very nicely with his wife.

I couldn't hear too much, but I think they were saying they expected a child soon.

I didn't say a thing to anyone.

It was their business.

Not mine.

And again time passed.

Benny used to come to me before going into the office and said, "Howdy."

His office was close to my locker.

He was not a mechanic.
He was some kind of manager.
Always clean and well-dressed.
I guess his wife was taking good care of him.
Because I was black like him, he seemed to likeseeing me.
For a few weeks, Benny didn't show up at the office.
When he finally came in he seemed like a different man.
Distressed, nervous, in a quarreling mood, agitated.
He had a fight with the boss.
For no reason.
But the boss didn't say anything.
That was strange.
The boss was merciless.
He would fire you immediately.
You know?
People talked that his wife gave birth to a white baby.
Real white.
Extremely white.
He was jealous, depressed, and his fairy-tale life was in ruins.
He had to make decision.
He didn't have the courage yet.

The lady who worked in the office and knew everything told a lot.

"Benny couldn't have children. It wasn't his wife's fault. It was his!"

The doctor had told them a long time ago.

And then his better half decided to have child for herself because time was running out.

She quickly found a big white man and started fucking.

Benny was at work.

Busy!

It was not too hard.

Soon the kid came like a curse on Benny.

She said simply, "What can I do? I badly need a child. My child."

That was the dilemma.

To be fair, she deserved a child.

Life is short, and it's hard not to have somebody.

To be all alone.

Benny understood all that.

But the jealousy kept eating him from in side. He couldn't sleep, couldn't eat, and didn't care about sex anymore.

I understood quickly why he had changed so much.

His life had become a long and painful struggle!

In the end, he proposed her to adopt a black child.

She categorically refused.

I got one black, you.

I don't need another one.

Benny never divorced her.

And the drama started to subside.

Benny's mother said that it would be better for him and his wife to move to another area and tell people he married her with child.

He was left with a great trauma.

Incurable.

## CHAPTER 26

# BILL MEETS MR. GLENN AGAIN

While he was crossing the street, Bill saw Mr. Glenn in the police car.

He invited him for a chat.

Mr. Glenn said, "I couldn't even if I wanted it. I'm on a mission now."

They set up a meeting for next Thursday.

They met and started to exchange recent news.

Mr. Glenn was very well informed.

He knew stuff I hadn't heard about.

I was very curious to learn some fresh news.

Mr. Glenn was relaxed and ready to start.

He asked me, "Did you hear about the latest crime in Texas? A black man shot mafia-style a white police officer! In spite of all the terror with the racism, authorities had to recognize that is a racial crime. A guy called Miles. There is no excuse now. What's happening now has been prepared by OBAMA a long time ago. These are the fruits of the plan."

"The Total War Against the Police initiated by OBAMA, Eric Holder, Al Sharpton, and di Blasio started bearing good fruit. That's what they wanted, to terrorize the police, to treat them like a doormat, incapable of organized action, resist the senseless riots and social chaos. That is power.

"But there is something that OBAMA and his gang didn't take into account. It's the state of quiet opposition. White people and even some black are starting to hate this politics of racism in action. When there isn't the slightest excuse for so many racial crimes. When the poor policemen are hunted in broad daylight by blacks and cowardly eliminated, no honest American will accept that. And all of them look at OBAMA with disdain."

I said, "Yes, I remember the horrible racial crime in New York. The black guy who came from another state to murder the two policemen had been instructed to kill and given all information how to quickly find the police car location, the timing, and the modus operandi. The world knows it was organized crime. Even his suicide is very suspicious. Black guy will do anything but do not commit suicide."

Mr. Glenn then said, "And planned death will soon hit even white people. It is planned. Tens, hundreds of white people will be killed in cold blood by blacks. Isn't that racism? It's a sad truth that cannot be kept hidden anymore, because it is racism.

"During the Ferguson riots, a white young man, a tourist from Europe, was there to visit a relative. Not being from here, he didn't know to beware of black men, and he was beaten to death in front of his aunt, without any reason and with barbaric hate. They bashed his head in with some big hammers. The poor boy died in hospital. No crime is justified. Life is above everything. And I can give you hundreds of examples. Pretty soon the whites will understand what the Liberals are preparing for them. And that's when the situation will calm down."

I said out loud, "Something must be done real soon. The whites are so stupid. Racism is a lie meant to agitate the black against some whites who haven't even heard of racism, they don't see anywhere, live in peace with others, regardless of color or creed. What a big misfortune for America. The higher-ups want war not peace in America. In any moment and place in the world, people have disputes, offend each other or ask the police for help. We can't just generalize that is racism.

"People fight and then they make up and its' their business. It's possible, very possible that one white person may not like a black person. So what?"

We only live once, and we should all live as we like.

Racism is like communism, socialism, fascism.

Trying to force everyone to be the same.

It's very hard because you can't force yourself to love someone else.

Any love must be conquered by efforts.

Now things are fast getting out of control.

The elections are the main cause the Liberals are restless and poison the atmosphere which used to be peaceful.

The police are armed and they can help efficiently reestablish public order.

They are our only hope.

With their special training and love of justice and fairness they can protect us.

Nobody!

Nobody else.

Destroying the police with diabolical perseverance and turning it in a powerless entity is a clear sign that for the whites everything is lost.

Blacks are not racist.

They mind their own daily business and like to befriend everyone.

Now you can see in the streets there are people from all continents and countries.

They speak all the languages of the planet.

They came here for a better life.

They, as well as us, are not racist.

Only if you really want to invent it for some purpose.

The whites in America want peace and equality for all.

And they regard peace of mind as great treasure.

Nobody wants to lose the rights and liberties that were so hard to get for some lies.

There will always be people who want to have nothing to do with others.

Even the most ferocious racism is not going to change them.

I propose that OBAMA has the guts to clearly define this racism.

To enable us to see clearly when something turns into racism.

To see if it is real in America.

It is not good to pile up lies on top of the honest hard working people.

And let's be clear.

Only whites are racist.

Actually racism was invented against the whites.

No black person can be a racist.

But this a big and false truth.

What can you say about the case in Texas?

We can no longer ignore lies and half-truths.

The people have had enough of OBAMA's tales

If there is a terrorist, that is OBAMA!

Ever since he took power he's been restless.

Agitating everyone.

Frantically playing the racism card.

You know the Occupy Wall Street riot.

Day and night young people went to a park in Manhattan.

For many months they terrified the city.

They were making an infernal noise.

Drums were deafeningly beaten and a left ofpeople left their homes to get a normal life.

They were yelling and howling about how much money is on Wall Street and why not give it to them.

Even on Fox News, an extremely intelligent white young man explained why we need a revolution in America.

It's simple.

"The state should provide everything for free."

"The guy was very good."

The state should provide them with housing, cars, food, medication, money for trips, in a word, everything they need.

And the same for his kids.

He was politely asked, "Who is going to pay because the state doesn't produce anything? It has only the taxes collected the people who work."

He mumbled something confusing:

"The money people on Wall Street."

It's clear that nobody is going to pay for some people to just sit and do nothing.

This young, intelligent guy was pretty sure that somebody must pay all his expenses.

Because he is entitled to do nothing and only benefit.

Who told them that kind of stupid things?

Who deceives them with economic equality, high hourly pay, and rights that can only be obtained with hard honest work?

Who?

Agitators handsomely paid by the Liberals deceiving people with their false and dangerous slogans.

They said they found out who's got the money!

They started to ask for redistribution immediately.

In that park of horrors, they were instigated not to go home or give up in any way. They had doctors and nurses checking up on them, pizza delivered, and paid by the agitators, hot coffee, and even some pocket money.

Well, the money came from a guy called George Soros, a comrade who enthusiastically supported them with his big money.

Everything had been approved from high up.

There was permanent sex.

Did you know?

They're young and they need it.

Under those tents, oh gully, what was going on?

They were shouting on cue all kinds of slogans.

Untrained, uneducated, idiot agitators told them to shout, "Hooray! Hooray! Hooray!"

We know who sucks everything!

We know who's got all the money!

The Jewish!

Or something like that!

That was the end of their underground movement!

They were woken up from their sweet sleep at six o'clock in the morning with freezing-cold waterhose, cleaning up that miserable place with garbage and unwashed people.

All their tents disappeared in the garbage trucks and nobody whispered a thing!

And the guys went home to watch the news on TV!

Who did that?

Police.

And Soros and the higher-ups lost by lying some youth.

And who saves us from the impromptu revolutionaries?

Only the police. Nobody else could scatter them away.

The higher-ups and Soros lost against justice and normality.

Does your OBAMA know it?

A pitiful police is all he wants now.

Americans, wake up till it's not too late.

America needs a powerful and just police like itneeds air to breath.

A police that will protect us all.

And that shall never kill an innocent.

Only police can save America.

What happened in Texas will happen daily from now on.

And not only policemen.

Soon it will be whites turn.

I said that 60 percent of blacks detest him because of his lying racism invented against the whites.

We know that for love of power some people became tyrants, criminals, beasts, and stepped everything under foot.

Read the history of England, France, Russia, China, and so on, even today in a civilized world such situations come up.

Look at Venezuela, North Korea, and black Africa and Arab countries.

I watched the news in horror.

I was a bit more confident in America's future.

Mr. Trump made very optimistic declarations.

Police must always be ready to defend us all.

Absolutely everyone.

And social order must be protected before anything else.

Even the police was more courageous and clearly declared.

Even with OBAMA's Permanent War Against Police, we the police officers will not give up doing our duty to America!

Sheriff Clark of Milwaukee said these days on Fox News that all the bad things appearing now in the police force are due to OBAMA.

So who has the blood of the innocent policemen on his hands?

Innocent blood is also on the hands of Eric Holder, Al Sharpton and mayor di Blasio.

Shame on them.

May God punish them for their pre-planned murders?

He said he would send a representative to the funeral of these victims.

I thing he will give up.

American policemen and honest citizens no longer tolerate blatant lies and perversion.

How does it work, you and your gang murder policemen and then you pretend you have no idea?

I am sure that your representative will be booed again and discredited by the dignified police officers of America.

You'd better keep there and try to stop the misfortunes you bring daily on America.

The white and black youth who believes in OBAMA's help have subscribed to all the revolutions.

The same guys in the Occupy Wall Street movement were chanting "Death to police!" or "Don't shoot!" or "Black lives count!"

And someone is paying them to keep the ready for the next coming event coming soon.

Now I'm thinking that for the six Baltimore policemen it is better in jail that being killed like dogs in the street.

Pretty soon many policemen will start looking for another job.

Even my dad could have worked somewhere else.

We would have been happy together now.

Better think about submitting your resignation.

America will appreciate that.

Finally, something normal.

# CHAPTER 27

# JIMMY, MR. JASON, AND KARL MARX

Walking in front of the main office at the university campus, Jimmy met Mr. Jason.

Delighted to see him again, Mr. Jason invited him in his office and offered him coffee.

Jimmy is an athlete and politely declined.

Mr. Jason started, "Last time when we spoke about racism, I was very angry and even violent. Saturday I went to a park with some good friends."

We played ball.

I discussed about racism with them.

Almost all of them clearly stated they don't see any racism in America.

All of them have a family and kids and enjoy a very good life.

Racism is a doctrine designed to defend the blacks against the whites.

Even OBAMA, who does a many good things for the blacks, should revise this racism thing.

Nowadays, many blacks have a job, houses, a good income, and enjoy a nice life.

Certainly any president wants all members of society to enjoy a decent living.

But practically it is impossible.

Socialism was a golden dream but huge, huge, huge disappointment dream a very comprehensive disillusion!

Think about it!

Each person to have a job, a house, a secure income, and never worry about tomorrow.

But that socialism was huge failure.

In Russia, in Cuba, in Venezuela, in China, and so forth.

Everywhere where it appeared, this socialism brought only losses, sufferings, misfortune, millions of shortages of all kind, political terror, arrests, deportations, practically an inefficient system against common sense and common people.

There were some people who travelled far away countries to fight and killed innocent people for the victory of socialism that definitely proved to be a total and inhuman system politic.

One of them is di Blasio, the mayor of New York, who aims high and wants to soon become the president of the Unites States.

Socialism is an old idea.

And Jimmy added: "Tommaso Campanella wrote a book *Walled City of the Sun,* where he is exalting the virtues of Socialism.

That theory is beautiful only in fairy tales.

Real life has demonstrated in all instances absolute in all instances that Socialism is a total failure, something that can't be done and stands, no chance.

But later the Karl Marx, a German Jewish, wrote a book *The Manifesto,* in which concentrated all ideas about socialism and using the dialectic, a genius creation by the greatest German philosopher, Emanuel Kant, succeed to lie people about the great and incredible advantages of it, luring others to build it.

In this way, Karl Marx based on his dreams, fantasy or lies created the most criminal, abdominal, terrorist, inhuman societies, installing in power the dictators which brought the humiliation, lack of any kind of right, a life of all kind of normal needs, a generalized corruption, lack of interest to work to produce something, destroying the religion, the traditions, the respect for the human being. And any hope to better life was violently and brutally reprimanded in a huge area of special campus, very well watched were fast built anywhere to calm forever people who were ready to die for a little change for better in their life. Humiliation, denunciation, imprisonment in the middle of the night with the slightest explanation, or total disappearance and no smallest right to ask officials for explanations lead to a society of huge and permanent fear and alienation.

There is a simple question, "How have these kind of societies collapsed even if the dictators opposed desperately?"

Simple answer: the socialism or communism is a big, big lie, and step-by-step, people understood the hoax!

---

It is true some tricky people kind of so to say political leaders still try now to cheat people here in USA about a special human socialism good for all or special one they are gifted to build, but all are lies, lies, lies and all what they want is the political power that will install new dictatorship, and you will pay a hard price for being stupid to believe them!

Russia ran away from socialism, China drastically changed its entire policy.

Socialism: It's a shame but simply does not work.

A theory to fool the world.

But the sly-dog socialist American politicians will try all the times according to the principle, "If I did not trick people today, I will trick them tomorrow, so? Never give up. Every day one stupid guy will be born."

And very decided members of Tricky Party like Sanders, Alexandra on occasion, or many candidates to bid Presidential race K. Amy, K. Harris, Gilibrand, C. Booker and many others will never give up looking for power. That is all they want, never even taking care of simple people.

How is it possible the Democrat Candidate for the precedence, Bernie Sanders, to prove very clear how insensitive, detached and perverse he is! After seeing a recent picture from a Russian Country in which a long, long, long line with very sad, unhappy people waited so quietly in front of a bakery shop to buy bread, Mr. Bernie Sanders, very relaxed said, "It is very good for people to wait hours in front of a bakers shop for bread! It is good for people. What is wrong?"

So this miserable, lying, perverse Democrat wants to be the President of America? The Democrats, all of them know very well what Socialism really will bring to American people. No way! This is why they never attack politically the Venezuelan Maduro. For what? They plan for America the same future like in any other socialist countries!

And as if it was not enough he was very decided and categorical, flat, clear, point-blank about his hidden inhuman, criminal terrorist intentions after taking the power

In front of many people during a rally, when a lady reporter asks him about his policy in terms of population in poor countries or any areas, Bernie S without any shame said:" Yes! We have a clear and tough program to limit the birth in poor countries and anywhere is needed"

So his clear program to limit number of new born is a clear INHUMAN AND PAINFUL PROGRAM.

The Democrat party is a terrorist party promoting such racist ideas, very much used against people, by Stalin, Lenin, Hitler and so forth.

Why Mr. Bernie did not offer a human chance trying to develop these poor countries with some help, some developing programs or investment? Why?

Because, he was and is a very criminal racist. In reality, he hates any human being. Just fancy this monster Sandi Bernie to take the power in America.

All population in the WORLD will be under his racist control.

God forbid to be elected!!!!

American people will never ever elect a president so relaxed and pitiless who is very decided to interdict too many women to enjoy being a mother or too many men to enjoy being a father

And how to achieve this birth control?

Forcing men to be castrated forever, physically or chemically, or may killing new born or put women in campus or how? Or exterminated this population by armed attack, poisoning, or starvation.

His criminal mind work fully against people.

Or in any country he will decided very relaxed and categorically who to have kids or not to have kids? From now on I will call Sandier Bernie TOVARISHTY STALINA !!!!

And all members of Democrat party, a party known as DO NOTHING PARTY think in the same way.

Now willy-nilly you Mr. Shit Bernie Sanders exposed yourself and your Democrat Party how much of a perverse, dangerous, liar you are! Shame! Shame again for your shit smelling Democrat Criminal Party! And why Alexandra on Ocasio Cortes and all shit Democrats if they are so skilled, do not use their special magic wands to transform Venezuela into a free, rich, and happy country?

We know now all the lying, terrorist, anti-American Democrats wish desperately is to bring in America a great Country a perfect glossy poverty to punish people for their good life and liberty like their big leader, Karl Marx!

Ah! The power is so sweet, so why not keep trying?

How stupid ridiculous and damaging idea to build a society, something like in China. "Cultural revolution", using only "Green energy deal".

Or a strange and big hoax idea they promise to bring everything free to all!

Free school, free houses, free transportation, free health care, free food, free items and why not my Alexandra's pussy free. By the top of stupidity, they encourage people to stay home in trips or vacation since the wonderful Socialism will pay everything for them, if they do not like going to work!

And to no surprise, these fantasy ideas were quickly embraced by all Democratic members.

Why?

For sure Karl Marx was totally confused creating such philosophy about Socialism, the Golden Future of humanity. Karl Marx was unable to understand very simple correlation between a very good life and the personal people wealth! A prosper Society is only one in which people make real profit and personal wealth by working hard and responsibly! If people wait from Socialist Government all for free, free, free or go to vacations, waiting others to work hard from them, as idiot Alexandra's on Occasion Cortez offered them in exchange for her political elections, the future is the one all these Socialist countries experience now! And Karl Marx was very confused how the Socialist countries will exist without respecting any law or traditions. Any law was imposed on the mercy of any boss. Democrat Anti American, wake-up!

During two Trump years, a very successful presidential time, to their huge shame, the Democrats did not offer anything good or constructive than "resist or opposed or obstruct and sabotage any initiative", like handicapped people and a huge permanent hatred for American people, proving that they are really impotent or empty and constipated mind so they run desperately and embrace any stupid, illogical or ridiculous ideas. Democrats prefer and enjoy for the death of America rather than success! Why do Democrats hate the real success of America?

Firstly all Democrats are very modest people, under taught control of SOROS George.

This huge, scaring, incredible, unjustified, unseen in the world HATRED is a normal expression and consequence of Hussein Al Barak Osama's hatred against white American people!!!

Secondly Democrats understood very fast and they proved that, they are unable to compete with so great President Mr. Trump, a real Patriot, Genius, Honest, and Real Humanist. Democrats are feeling so miniscule, so dirty, so ridiculous, so modest, so insignificant, and so shameful, close to him. So they need desperately to lie and make waves to trick American people.

Really, Democrats have nothing to offer just a scaring perspective of Socialism.

Some know that they are no patriots but they are crazy to get the power by all means!

The farce to IMPEACH the best possible of America President is a very shameful act of National Treason!

—⋙—

This goes without saying that Democrats are not American Patriots Party! In their huge infinite and unjustified hatred for the president's success, they hate the Republicans or any one that voted for Trump. Just remember the Hillary words "all are a bunch of deplorables". And when you see the faces and red eyes of Democrats like low IQ Maxine W, Adam Schiff, Green and so forth, you realize how dangerous they are for the American people.

Recently, a second-hand actor, poor actor J Smollet in Chicago was caught in a very shameful lie, creating a huge and unexpected farce. He soon will go to jail for lying to the American society in such a dangerous manner.

No way this is the Democrats work now and in many other similar situations.

So OBAMA, Hillary, Pelosi, Maxine, Green, Cunning and practically all Democrats who approved such a fascist manner to fight for power must keep liable or responsible! The Democrat party must be put out of society and out of laws now! Hatred for Trump is clearly a hatred for any American people.

And their constipated mind cannot see the simple and logical connection between president Trump's success and wealth of the American people!

Any Trump success is to the best benefit of the American people, not for president Trump. Mr. Trump already has lots of money, so he doesn't need to take a cent for himself. He does not take a dollar from Government, as his job is made extremely difficult due to the Anti-American Democratic party.

I have never seen in human history such an act of patriotism!

Already millions and millions of American patriots think seriously to elect Mr. Trump President for life! Why? Because they are scared that Democrats will take the Power in White House!

A president to work so hard for free!

Jimmy continues: "No doubt Democrat party became a very terrorist party, and they publicly support ideas of political assassinations as a normal procedure to annihilate any political opponent. They are very tough. Nobody to contradict or oppose them."

It seems to be clearly very fanatic followers of Lenin the Russian socialist leader philosophy.

"If you are not with me, you are against me, and so you have to die!"

No compromises!

Democrats use their power in very destructive ways. There is no positive or progressive way for American people.

A party that in any moment in any action is full of ridicules, hatred, and stupidity.

For sure they lost connection with the reality of the American people.

They made a fool of them all the time.

I used to be a Democrat but after four years of confusion and understanding how dangerous they are for the American people, I quickly moved to the Republican party and many others like me did the same.

Showing so much hatred against someone who got their power for a while is shameful and very scary!

Doesn't matter now as Trump is in office. They filed their souls, hands and actions with terrible feeling of revenge.

American people elected Mr. Trump as president, not for his sexual life or for his good money.

America really did not look for a Saint or Pope as president.

He is better than a homosexual or pedophile guy.

Mr. Trump is a very normal man who loved a lot of girls. He is not concerned about making money like the presidents before him.

Democrats, I ask you to remember Biblical story. When people were ready to stone a woman for husband infidelity, Jesus said: Throw the first stone if you have never sinned or made a mistake in your life.

So wake up Pelosi, Hillary, Schiff, Cunning and all members of this compromised party! So it's no surprise why Democrats behave like handicapped people.

Their infinite huge amount of hatred against the American president for his incredible success, represents the Socialist practice where any successful man will be very much punished and brought to his modest place very fast.

Mr. Jenson said, "And I am really very impressed how smart and intelligent our President is. Now Mr. Trump ignores this ridicule party.

—⚋—

Capitalism is the best for the people.

It is certainly not perfect.

But a thousand times better than the lie and hoax socialism Karl Marx created.

When somebody works for the money and this money allows him to live a decent, good, and comfortable life enjoying all the facilities offered by a free society, that is what you call personal happiness.

Capitalism offers unlimited opportunities.

Not all people are equal.

It's very hard to believe this kind of nonsense.

Yes, people should be equal before justice, authorities.

They have rights and nobody is allowed to break them.

In any way.

Jason continues: "I am a black in America, but it is hard to believe there is another socialist country in the world to offer to me my great real life I really live now."

Jimmy says: "So Mr. Karl Marx, to my mind, should be judged postmortem in an international court for his millions and millions of victims because he created a very lying philosophy that people will incredible benefit of a socialism."

I already mentioned above the chain of long and incredible kind of all possible and hard to imagine huge sufferings people experienced just for a false and lying criminal theory a stupid fantasy of a man confused himself about what socialism really offered.

Nowadays some strange and uneducated politicians try to trick the naïve people so good this lying and impotent Socialism will be for them.

These lying politicians I think do have no courage to answer a simple and fascinated question in front of their honest people: if the socialism is as they try to trick naive people, is so beneficial for human beings, so good, so correct, so wished, so very much wanted, bringing 100 percent happiness social and economical equality and wealth for all, why did this glorious socialism collapse so shamefully in all countries where it was installed by revolutionaries of profession like di Blasio, our mayor, who fought with the gun to help countries to install it?

The countries like Russia, Poland, Hungary, Romania, Czechoslovakia, Bulgaria, and Germany desperately crushed this great socialism forever.

And ridiculously the couple of socialist countries remain like Cuba, North Korea, or Venezuela and so forth represent a very hard and sad and undesired place to live normally. In these remaining socialist countries, the people are permanently under a very bestial control made clear by Secret Services and punished in an inhuman manner.

So my real idea for the need of an international court to judge and convict Mr. Karl Marx to death penalty for abominable horrible crimes against humanity makes perfect sense.

People have a right to know and no to be tricked by politicians of profession to admit a socialist system for their countries.

What does capitalism do?

Now I live in capitalism, and believe me, it would be a social disaster if socialism came over us.

That's where the Liberals are wrong.

Humans are the most valuable capital.

But they need to be motivated to work, to make the effort, physical or intellectual.

We must openly admit that some people do not want to work.

Black or white, that is the situation.

A smart society must know.

And that's where the trouble starts.

Socialism is for those people who do not want to work but want to receive money, goods, and advantages without any effort on their part, being pleased with very, very modest life.

That way, in its desperation to survive, socialism makes all kinds of efforts to meet everyone's modest very modest necessities.

And you get the collapse of socialism.

The Liberals are crazily in love with socialism.

By offering all kinds of assistance, they created a class of people dependent on the Liberals.

The Liberals give them money, and they must vote for the Liberals.

Do you remember when Harry said in the Senate that all poor people must come to the Liberals!

And he was publicly very angry that an illegal immigrant signed up with the Republicans!

Illegal immigrants, all go to Democrats!

Liberals are helping them.

For their historical vote.

Right?

Logical.

The fact that power is sweet and you must keep it at all costs is another story.

And that's how we get to racism.

I said real fast, "Why are there riots after riots? Why there are so many people going out in the street and shouting all kinds of slogans? And why in this permanent atmosphere of fight against an indefinite enemy so many policemen are being killed?"

Remember when I said that there is no racism in America?

Yes!

Racism doesn't exist.

That's why it must be created.

That is the big problem of the Liberals.

In order to retain the power, racism is necessary.

As I was saying, capitalism is better than any other form of government.

But capitalism offers an unlimited number of options

And you must choose one and start working for your well-being.

That's it!

You must work.

Not sit and wait for the dole.

Who are you?

Why should another one sweat and work hard for you?

Well?

If not, then you go out and riot.

And scare the shit out of those who work so that they know you need your social assistance, and God forbid if they don't send it in time.

Because otherwise!

You'll get in trouble.

We must logically admit that not all the people have a job!

That not each human being can work.

Therefore, not too many need social assistance.

And capitalism thought about that.

There are plenty of social assistance programs.

Nobody starves here.

There many things to be said about the homeless people.

But they are not so many.

The homeless people can't work, are sick, and cannot live comfortably in a shelter protecting them from the cold, hunger, anything.

But they don't need the shelter.
They feel like in prison there.
They have a schedule that must be followed.
And they don't like it.
If they did like it, they would have their own home, a family.
They feel good in total freedom living in the street and under bridges and in parks.

But the number of services is dropping rapidly.
Friends of mine told me they have to look for a job elsewhere because positions are being terminated.
Well!
That's a government problem.
Too many regulations are simply choking small businesses.
Yesterday a city inspector, one of di Blasio's people, came over and gave a twenty thousand dollar fine to a small business owner who can hardly stay in business.
Why?
For not paying OBAMA's Medicare to his four employees.
The owner first called his employees and explained the situation to them.
Then he asked them if they agree to apply for part-time jobs.
They all applied because otherwise all they were going home.

Honestly, this policy against small businesses is totally wrong.
These days you can see higher than ever numbers of small businesses closing shop in America.
They all join the ranks of unemployed people.
It's really scary to see on every street many stores with signs like Space for Rent or Out of Business.
And large windows taped with paper.
I said that soon Labor Day was coming.

What Labor Day?

Who's still working nowadays?

Only in government buildings.

Not to mention the poor employees who lose any chance of making some money.

That's the rub.

And the higher-up bosses just don't get it.

They keep on invoking racism.

If you don't have a steady source of income, you start thinking of ways to make money at any cost.

Let's move now to foreign affairs.

How about the agreement with Iran?

The Jewes don't agree with it not at all!

Can you sign an agreement without Israel's accord?

They know very well that Iran wants them dead!

Erased from the map!

All allies are scared!

How can you allow the atomic bomb to someone who shouts "Death to America" and "Down with America"?

Same thing about Israel.

I don't get it?

Mr. Jason said, "Foreign policy just like domestic policy are not easy for him. Problems are piling up, and a fast decision is needed."

But we were discussing about something else.

"I hope you understand that racism doesn't exist and that the Liberals should finally get it and stop this nonsense. What do you say of the death of police officers one after the other?" I asked Mr. Jason.

A bit embarrassed, he tried to avoid answering the question.

I didn't insist.

He said it's a tough question, and he doesn't like to explain something that everyone understands.

He only said, "This way many friends will start looking for other friends. It's not good at all! Pretty soon the police will get so small you won't see it anymore?"

You know we talked about racism.

I and many others like me know that there is no such thing in America.

For some people OBAMA is pretty good.

He maintained social assistance programs at a high level.

But he has also impoverished America more than anyone before him!

The debt he accumulated talks for itself!

Many were helped and benefitted from that.

He would do anything to attract more votes.

Care for the other is care for his power.

I voted for him the first time and the second time.

We will vote him as many times as he tells us to.

He is our president and we feel protected.

But I got to admit many things could have been done better.

And that maybe another more experienced president will raise America higher.

OBAMA diminished America as much as he could.

I don't think he did intentionally.

Too much responsibility of this position for just one man.

There are also shortcomings.

After Mr. Bush as the time goes by, who made a huge mistake invading IRAQ, proving he was no too good politician, another came to WH.

Now a Black Muslim, who strongly promised to REMAKE America which finally, after 8 years, meant, without any doubt, to destroy America?

Hussein Al Barak, was born in Kenya and late very late come to America via Chicago.

He never got a serious school. He never got a serious job. And he stolen money from SS by false documents used by his "Mike" called a wife.

Everyone knew Hussein is a homosexual, desperate to promote the LGBT in all directions.

I am married and I have kids. Any times my wife was pregnant this was a very happy event. So lots of pictures, videos and so forth were made to immortalize the moments. And tones of pictures for birthdays or any event like first walking steps, school and so forth.

Hussein and "Mike" were unable to produce or to present one single picture, in 16 years in their <SO TO SAY FAMILY > with the two their nice girls!!!???!!!???

There are many doubts that Hussein and Mike are the biological parents of the two nice girls.

Now is evident and very clear. Hussein Al Barak was born in Kenya, came illegally from INDONEZIA in USA via Chicago, doubts if he has American Citizenship yet. He experienced a very hard life full of lack of anything. Hussein Al Barak hated to death America making him a very anti patriot. Just before moving to WH he showed his criminal intentions. At his first inauguration he declared <<I REMAKE AMERICA >> and the most population in America are the <MUSLIM POPULATION > ;what is a huge devil intention statement. In his bad leading time he bought 2,500 terrorist men from Iran for <sleeping cells> with modern military equipment and granted them AMERICAN CITIZENSHIP in couple's hours. They are hidden on the American country, ready to help Hussein Al Barak if any.

President Trump thinks to soon deport them.

Hussein Al Barak SADAM and his "wife" Mike are Muslims affiliated with Muslim Terrorist Organizations around the world. His mentor David Duke educate him in spirit of violence, disregard for human being and to develop stronger and stronger relationship with Muslim criminal originations. During more than 20 years they were closely connected with the pastor Jeremiah Wright from Trinity United Church of Christ, who proved without any doubts they are MUSLIM.

It is still a big mystery, secret how was possible, this dirty family became first family for 8 years!!!???!!!???

And now we know that Hussein Al Barak Sadam Obama is a TRAITOR organizing a "COUP de Etat" against a very legally elected American President Trump J Donald.

We the people hope still hope that the American Justice will work and will put this criminal, liar Sadam Al Barak in his right place in JAIL. His time at WH was a very bad disastrous time for America.

He destroyed America and compromised America on the International Field.

I said very bravely.

I think that America must choose from now on only people with real life experience and true patriots.

At first sight, anyone can be president.

Only enjoying the advantages of the office is not enough.

History of America is full of good presidents.

But I don't think that the president OBAMA is happy when the whole world considers you the weakest most incompetent president ever.

I smiled sadly, and we parted ways amiably.

# CHAPTER 28

# JIMMY, ROGER, AND COURT FOR KARL MARX

Five months ago, a French family moved in the neighborhood.

The tall, handsome boy enrolled in the university program.

We met at the calculus course.

We introduced ourselves and started to chat.

His sister was very beautiful, and I liked her a lot.

But she had a boyfriend in Paris, who will coming over soon.

I tried to corrupt her without success.

I charmed her, talked to her. It was all a waste of time.

She refused to see me anymore.

I was surprised and admired her sincerity and honest life philosophy.

This can break any man's heart.

Roger's father was an engineer and worked for General Electric.

Their mother was ill, and that made them move to America for a special heart treatment.

Honestly, I have never seen their mother.

Only their father sometimes late in the evening.

One day I invited Roger to play some tennis.

I was interested in meeting Eugenie.

I was still hoping to win her heart.

We were chatting and ended up talking about politics.

He said that his father has no appreciation for what's happening in the USA now.

The Liberals are impossible and the Republicans have no program.

And that the general situation is so explosive because of racism.

He wrote many articles, but he was afraid to publish them because he didn't know if the First Amendment was still respected.

The First Amendment of the American Constitution is still respect indeed.

He wanted to consult a lawyer, but he was caught up in his work.

He believes that the American government doesn't have the slightest consideration for the country's Constitution.

He would like to publish, but he's afraid he will be arrested, thrown in jail, or loses the American citizenship he obtained two years ago, or deported to France for racism, which is very fashionable these days and which is wrong and a big lie.

Or he could be shot mafia-style by the special forces created by you know who!

He wouldn't like to go back to France because of his mother's illness and special treatment.

Because his mind is still fresh and unpolluted by the poisonous in America, he sees clearly and precisely what is going on.

When he saw that OBAMA had already condemned the Ferguson policeman well before the trial he understood that things are not good.

As you know the policeman was found not guilty, and the young Brawn wanted to take the policeman's gun and shoot him.

But that's another story.

Having Holder in charge of the Justice Department and now his Loretta Lynch, the Liberals will start a new trial for convicting Williams, the police officer.

Soon you'll see the demonstrations the Liberals will organize.

The entire America will come out in the street supposedly for true justice not like that one of last year that respects the American laws!

America has now two justices.

One correct and just and one true justice for Liberals.

And the verdict, which is already printed, shall sentence him to life in prison a simple policeman who was in self-defense.

Those are small matters, and Holder was smiling when he received from Congress a well-deserved nonconfidence vote for repeated failure and contempt in applying the law.

Now his clone, Loretta Lynch, the new Justice Department chief has the same tasks.

You'd see that pretty soon they would reopen with much pomp the Ferguson trial.

Victory is assured.

The worst part is that OBAMA's Total War Against Police has succeeded perfectly.

The war was won fast, and the whites of America have lost the slightest chance of being respected.

The blacks showed America that they won without any doubt and America had better behave or else it will be in big trouble.

The police tried to defend themselves and stop the diabolical plans to kill policemen like some troublesome flies.

They have lost all hope.

Best thing for them would be to look for another job or increase the rate of police officers killed on duty.

How is it possible that a well-known drug dealer in Baltimore be rewarded $6.4 million without a trial and a court judgment?

That reward that defying common sense proves that the State Department does not have the dignity of facing reality.

Loretta Lynch doesn't have time to waste with a long and fair trial.

All six policemen are simply guilty in advance, and it is only a question of time before they are convicted.

That young Gary had no job and no interest in having one.

He was arrested in a place where the mayor found out that was a daily meeting place for all the drug dealers.

And the mayor demanded that practice got to stop.

The police went there, and the nice, lively fellow who was a known and dedicated client to the police refused to surrender, took out his knife, and ran away.

None of the policemen though of shooting him or beating him.

The policemen chased after him and arrested him as ordered by the smart mayor and died in the police car without any proof that the policemen hit him or touched him.

To be fair, there is no evidence to arrest the six policemen.

It's a big abuse perpetrated by the Justice Department that acted alone upon the chief's order.

OBAMA quickly acknowledges the reward amount to be given to the drug dealer's family and approved immediately.

This young black man weighing over a hundred and seventy pounds will receive $6.4 million dollars representing twice and a half his weight in gold.

The police were overwhelmed and destroyed and exasperated by that decision.

Certainly the Baltimore mayor's office arranged the affair with the Department of Justice with OBAMA's consent.

When the proposal, if there was one, was made by the Baltimore mayor's office, who could say it was too much?

Why the racism was invented?

Understanding the troubles waiting for them, the police declared that the reward was obscene, which is huge knowing that they have been in a frightening situation for some time due to OBAMA's Total War Against Police.

Any police officer will become a valuable target intentionally sought by the blacks to make a ton of easy money in a few seconds.

That is the policy of terrorists who told their recruits with suicide vests killing many innocent people that their families will be compensated with a lot of money after their heroic death!

Why did OBAMA ask for such huge sum of money for the reward?

Is he paying one cent of his money?

He has no problem of taking tax payer money and consequently he will increase taxes to recuperate the reward sum.

When the police say that the reward is obscene it means that some blacks will do whatever they want against the police and the social disaster has been approved and nobody and nothing will stop them because money talks.

My father, who's a notorious humanist, said, "Each life is important and nobody must fall victim to force, hate or injustice. Nobody should die unjustly. Each human being has one life that is his and his own. But each person in this world has a personal life and he should live it as he can. The value of an individual is measured in what he brings to society, how much he helps society progress, how he contributes to social wealth through science, inventions, everyday work. Society values the good, correct and hardworking people. Society creates opportunities for everyone."

And society protects people regardless of religion, sex, education, status, color.

Society treats everyone equally.

But equality in legal terms.

Each person in the American society is treated as equal by police, justice, government, and absolutely all his/her rights are respected.

But society also takes care to reward, encourage, and honor those who are good members.

The ones that mind their own business and do their job.

# THE DEATH PENALTY FOR KARL MARX

Those people will never be arrested, taken into police cars, convicted in justice, or thrown in jail.

Those people are a model to follow and the society treasures them.

Therefore, a person's value resides in the work and earnestness in treating the needs of society.

Basically, man is priceless.

His/her life is above everything.

But that is the clean, honest, great, fair, and desired side of American society.

I asked my father why there are jails, police, crimes, drugs, innocent victims and so much pain, sadness and moral decay?

Why are jails full of people?

Even OBAMA said that there are more blacks in prisons than in school!

Why do we need pain and suffering in the American society?

The police was created because of the desperate need to defend the good people from the bad!

The police are trained to work for everybody.

To defend everybody, whenever necessary.

The police are called night and day to defend our interests and our rights.

What happened in Baltimore with the reward represents total lack of respect for the concept of value in the American society. Absolutely all the Liberals decided to compensate the family of the black young man for his death in the police car, although he had been arrested for selling drugs and resisting arrest and threatening policemen with a knife and running away.

That way the Liberals will win millions of votes and will not lose the Power.

By compensating the black guy's family with such a huge sum of money, the Liberals are only after keeping the black population under control and offer them a good and convincing proof that they are the ones defending the blacks.

That's how whenever necessary, the blacks will go out in the street and set fire to police cars, vandalize stores, loot and break and create general panic and terror.

I hope that the Senate and the Congress will have the courage and political responsibility to firmly oppose that sort of rewards that represent nothing but corruption at the highest level.

And that's it.

The American democracy is dead!

The blacks and some whites will start thumbing their nose at the policemen who will be humiliated, insulted, discredited, beaten and disregarded in order to provoke them to defend themselves and thus be implicated in a situation that will quickly be called racism. They will take their guns and equipment and will dance around them and maybe a policeman who still have a spine will try to defend himself.

And tens of cameras arranged by Loretta Lynch's order will immortalize the moment and we will see the police drama unfold.

And they'll throw away money compensations to the smart black agitator who felt offended.

Loretta Lynch's Department of Justice in its parental care will make sure that each black person touched even by mistake by a policeman will immediately be generously compensated, because they have tons of money.

And many innocent policemen will be murdered in cold blood in broad daylight because the killers know they will be promptly released.

OBAMA is lying all the time.

Both in domestic politics and in foreign affairs.

Now in order how great a leader he is, the Pentagon started to falsify military reports regarding ISIS.

This terrorist organization, supposedly a State, is described as moderate and due to OBAMA's wise policy they allegedly lost ground and are weak and impotent.

Why do you think we pay taxes?

Just like that.

My father is very honest man and all his life abided by the law and respected everyone's rights.

He is not a racist and doesn't like politics.

He is a just a man and sees very well what's going on.

He told me that many times at work he deals with all kinds of people and that he cannot say that white or Chinas, European, or Latinos or blacks are different.

There is good and bad in everyone.

Nobody is perfect, but nobody is the worst either.

There is always room for improvement!

The problem sits with the Liberals who in their desperate clinging to power would do anything to agitate people on all occasions.

There are many who trust them and follow them obediently.

Racism does not exist and even the blacks feel humiliated by this racism.

OBAMA created it and scares the whites into avoiding to have any opinion on anything.

The whites are already finished.

For an honest man from the outside, from another country, it is crystal clear.

The Liberals want votes and must win again.

Millions of voters and Liberals are well entrenched in their positions.

The Republicans hold some power in the Congress and the Senate but are incapable of say anything against OBAMA.

The Republicans are respectfully serving OBAMA, and they will never do anything to anger him.

It's just a dance.

It's a kind of joke that they are working too hard, you know?

That is the real situation in America.

The racism invented by OBAMA, Al Sharpton, di Blasio, and the Liberals generally created the weakest and most incompetent society based on fear of telling the truth, criticizing and has raised the lie to the rank of truth and this will shortly lead to a coup d'état.

Now they are ready for elections in 2016.

Another scam.

Hillary must lose so that Biden wins.

Everything has been arranged for a long time.

If that guy wins, he will be another OBAMA.

The Republicans have a lot of candidates that are a laughing stock.

Now they are quarreling among themselves like there is no tomorrow.

Exactly what the Liberals want.

America is collapsing and that's what the Liberals need.

There is one candidate who is more advanced in polls but rest assured that the Liberals higher-ups plan will take him down.

He must be compromised, strongly slandered, ridiculed so that people make the better choice that is the Liberals.

Some of the ideas expressed by this Republican candidate are already closely watched by the Liberals and pretty soon we'll hear how evil he is and that people must not vote for him.

And soon Trump will be denounced as an intruder, a dangerous person.

The Liberals noise-making crew has already started slandering him.

Soon we will hear the following:

"Trump jumped over the garbage site of the city and disturbed all the birds that had just come to pick a fresh shipment, proving he total lack humanity."

"Trump thought out loud, and a lot of people heard him, that he wants to take a bath this evening."

"In his desire to get power, Trump forgot to take the elevator and used the stairs."

"Trump chased a homeless man for a nice colorful pair of socks."

"Trump is ready to do anything and he just ate a big pie in one bite."

"Trump is dangerous because he inadvertently stepped on a hardworking ant that was crossing the street to its children."

"Trump wants to climb into the plane without the fire escape ladder."

Liberals will always be vigilant and inventive.

But life will go on whether you like or not.

Who knows if the Liberals or the Republicans will be in power?

But I am hoping that a new generation of true politicians will follow and save what can still be saved.

I have a strange feeling if Mr. Trump will get the election the Democrats, with OBAMA, Soros, Hillary, di Blasio Mayor of New York, and so forth will make him a hard impossible hard life to oppose to his good program for American people.

God helps Mr. Trump to resist criminal actions against him and his family!

Many whites are very frightened by the presence of blacks.

Some of them told me that when they go to work, they say goodbye to their families as if they weren't coming back.

Many feel terrorized when a big stout black guy heads toward them.

They expect to be shot mafia-style.

Fear started to take over many people.

They are right in a way.

They easily shot experienced and highly trained policemen, and it would be really simple to shoot an inexperienced defenseless unarmed white guy.

How is it possible that the police could not find the Chicago criminals who shot a policeman the other day.

It is clear that the perpetrators are trained to avoid capture or detection and are hiding very well for future crimes.

You will see a vast amount of crimes coming.

In different states and city, it will look like random acts.

Anyway, the police understood exactly what is going on.

America wake up till it's not too late.

Now other nonsense.

Mohamed, a fourteen-year-old Muslim invented a big device with a lot of electrical wires and a clock inside, and he brought the device into his school.

Everything was fine, but when the poor students and the teachers saw the innovation with the wires and the clock, they freaked out and called the police.

Due to the relentless work of terrorists who with their wire and clock devices blew up and killed tens of thousands of innocent people, the world has developed a culture of fear and horror and terror.

Anywhere in the world, when people see a device with many wirers and a clock in the hands of someone called Mohamed, they will panic and automatically remember Paris and London subway bombings, the attacks in hotels, airplanes, and in Boston.

The poor people don't even think of racism.

They are only thinking how to save their life.

Somebody called the police who came very fast.

Just think what if that kid wanted to blow up the other students and the teachers.

Dramas, sufferings, and pains.

I am sure that if this Muslin came to school with his breakthrough invention and clearly explained what it was, nobody, absolutely nobody would have freaked out.

There something funny here.

Very funny!

We'll find out.

So the police came and took this contraption with wires and clock, immobilized Mohamed the Genius and possibly averted a great tragedy.

As it so happens it was all a big scare.

Thank God it was not a terrorist attack.

---

Everybody knows that terrorists use innocent children to blow up the infidels.

In America and in the world, there has been a permanent threat of terrorist attack since ISIS was overtly encouraged and every day new terrorist attacks take place…

The damaging thing is that OBAMA used this false terrorist attack to show that the policemen are stupid and idiots because they didn't have the intuition to understand what a great genius Mohamed was and consequently he will invite him to the White House to encourage him for the unexpected benefit of science.

The clock with its many wires was studied by specialists who discovered that the device is not in any way a breakthrough invention but was simply bought in a store for four or five bucks.

Therefore, the great breakthrough innovation of Mohamed the Genius is just another hoax and naming this boy a genius is ridiculous.

But there is something fishy here.

Did somebody prepare him to do it for racial benefits?

The police acted perfectly.

Very professional!

They received a call from a school, and they promptly went to the school to save victims of a possible terrorist attack.

They arrested Mohamed to make sure he cannot activate the clock with many wires and they investigated the device.

When they fast realized that there was no danger, they released the boy and started the investigation.

---

The police deserve praise and appreciation and gratitude.

Who else might have saved those children and teachers if there was real terrorist attack?

Therefore, police are not stupid and are not racist.

Respect the police. He is our only chance to be protected from troubles of any kind.

OBAMA's Total War Against the Police is not justified.

Hard to believe but now this Mohamed and his smart family decided that it is was not enough the terror brought in the school with this clock with many wires.

They expected to be rewarded with some change of no more than fifteen million dollars.

Smart! What to say?

---

And now will follow lots of troubles with the migrants that will start in all Europe many and endless terrorist's attacks and poor innocent victims have to pay for their brave leaders.

How it is possible that Markel from Germany, and Holland, Macron from France, and others, to be happy to receive so many migrants who are coming in endless waves?

They did not understand or care a little that these migrants came to revenge and to continue their saint and dear war. This is not a story or racism how someone would like to say fast.

They invaded and continue to invade Europe helped by some American millionaire like Soros or someone more, more, up.

Well, these are very poor man, so how to pay thousands of dollars for so nice trip?

You will see it very soon!

I am sorry for all dramas that will follow.

A very serious problem is now in actuality.

How to encourage millions of migrants to abandon and leave their countries as long as they have to be good citizenships and to stay in their countries and to fight for their countries not to come to Europe for begging food, a place to sleep or money, and eventually jobs!

Some are very violent and consider that this is their right?

So Europe to start giving them all they need?

This will be very soon a tough and hard judgment in the future!

They will be called cowards. So who to fight for their native country?

Who to help your country to be a good place for all their kin?

And how so easy, they gave up to their culture, traditions, language, and life for something totally new and different and hard to be admitted by their strict religion?

Many of them will suffer lot for these changes or will become strong radical Muslims and ready to fight the Europe!

—m—

What can you say about huge and unpardonable political mistakes made by Occident against the Arabian countries?

These countries live quietly their life. They are living in accordance with their precepts.

And what is wrong with it?

They have a very developed cult when is come to woman!

Never ever to touch or to try to touch their pussy!

Once you did it you are a dead man!

Everything till their pussy!

Here the Occident did not understand a jot!

They have a religion that is only their religion.

Their woman by ancient traditions has no too many rights, but she is very protected if and only if she is a woman that respects totally all required precepts, such as not to go out alone with unknown persons, not to have a lover out of her family, and so far, and a pile of rules.

Otherwise, the woman, she could be killed. She can pay for these mistakes with death. You know the Sharia rules!

By contrary the woman in democratic countries have all possible and impossible rights!

The democratic woman really can do all what she wants and no one will dare to stop her or to disturb her in some ways.

The police just wait for any kind of complaints.

Even some TV channels encourage the women to have at least one extra lover because the life is too short.

But the reverse of medal appears too.

Many men started considering the woman good chance to exploit her or give her too many rights and step-by-step, but surely this will bring her to a very developed sexual industry under million and millions of shapes!

Thousands of women from all over the world started having a special slave sexual life and hard very hard to escape from so incredible sufferings.

So they are valuing the woman in their way. These men by no means want democracy, which for them means total sexual liberty of their women!

They want to be and to remain their women's masters and any try to change their status is predestined to the fail.

They do not need of democracy to lose their right of being the boss! Period!

So the fight against the confused democracy, which wants to change their life, traditions, sexual practices, or morale and religion, must start very decided, and this democracy to be stop by all means!

All terrorist groups named so by us were created to stop a democracy they see or understand.

The terror of such kind of democracy unite them against any kind of invasion on their territories

And a real victory of Occident is far very far away and never possible.

Only an honest and clear recognition of their religion and morale and of their social practices sure can lead to a long peace term!

Even more, hard to believe, in order to weak the Occident, they organized and developed very perverse and even intelligent forms for resisting.

They suggest us to keep this democracy there in Occident.

For sure they never ever need such a thing!

Noooooo!

God forbid!

Finally is the case that the Occident to understand the reality and to stop any military aggression or any kind of attack against any Arabian country?

The peace to start even from this moment!

The only logic way for the Occident to influence in some way the Arabian society is only the education!

The education is the only and really option for the Occident.

Yes!

It takes time but it's really the smartest and possible one to affect their lives.

In rest only dramas over dramas of all kind and much very much sufferings in both sides!

—∽—

The world is full of sad things! The very newly and unexpected terrorist attacks clearly showed that the world never to forget about Muslims!

Even Muslims born in France or America remained the same permanent source of terrorism!

Father told me that innocent people will pay the audacity to live in France, USA, or any European country.

So everybody alone must do all possible in their power to protect them self and their family.

The government proved clearly that it is not capable to protect you and proved it many times, especially in the last terrorist attacks.

Everybody needs a gun for personal protection

Asking people to give up to weapons to protect them self the government convicted you to the death!

And is not fair anymore!

After so many victims and dramas, it is your right to protect yourself and to be ready.

No one knows when a new terrorist attack comes over you or your family!

All late regrets or sincere condolences have no chique as long as you are dead or a long period of huge sufferings hits you!

Why? And why?

In his huge desire to trick the innocent's people, OBAMA starts weeping, of course with crocodile tears.

Nowadays we know very well this man!

To the Paris, OBAMA totally ignored this huge and hard and very possible threat and tried to distract the attention from Muslims and to straighten attention to a very illusory and crass invention such as climate change!

It does not work!

The people understood perfectly!

If you die without reason because of Muslim terrorists only, so the climate change is a huge and unjustified and uninterested lie!

No long time ago the very prestigious company NASA publicly declared that the climate change is not true, and on the Antarctic Ocean, for example, the ice is increasing with an amazing speed and there is no reason to worry.

And no surprise a new Ice Age Era will soon start to come over to the planet and huge and hard winters and lots of cold will cover us.

So the government has to stop these many lies!

And OBAMA started a very desperate manner to protect the Muslims!

If you, OBAMA, are not capable to tell me who's the Muslim who will kill me soon, stop the lies!

Now OBAMA has desperately started to protect Muslims by all means!

The boss from Justice Loretta Lynch said clearly that nobody to try to say something about Muslims, so they will have to meet her power and special laws. Even if about the fourteen were killed and twenty-two were wounded were recently in San Bernardino in California.

---

And now we waiting that America started a terror life due to OBAMA's policy.

From now on daily lots of malls, subways lines, schools, offices will be closed because of fear of terrorist attacks.

This is the time for American citizens to close the mouth. Otherwise, they will see the devil with Loretta Lynch!

If you died or you are hard wounded in a terrorist attack, it is your lucky day.

The Great OBAMA will take special care to send to you on time sincere condolences because he is not capable of something else!

---

My dad often told me about the Liberals dedicated and blind wish to bring socialism to America.

They understand nothing of this illusory, lying, criminal, unjust, and fascist society!

In theory, socialism is perfect.

All equal, legally and economically.

It's a dream.

But a deceitful dream.

Life has proved that such a society is possible only on paper and in words not in everyday reality.

How many countries have built socialism with revolutionary enthusiasm and finally was blown in the wind.

Everybody knows that socialism is not possible.

That socialism is worse, a thousand times worse than capitalism!

Many countries gave it up or are on the way to give up that socialist deceit.

When socialism brings nothing but suffering, misery, arrests, death, deportations, prisons, bestiality, terror, uncertainty, treason, lies, indescribable abuses, inequality, lack of rights, lack of any human right, denouncements, hate, and deliberate ignorance of freedom of thought and religion, for whom is socialism good?

Oh! For the higher-ups who live a dream life on the backs of the many unfortunate ones.

I am looking in astonishment at the Liberal candidate Sanders and hundreds of other Democrats, who are determined to build socialism if he is elected president of America!

And thousands of people are following him!

How is it they don't understand the simple fact that socialism in practice is a great lie?

Now all leaders and top members of the Democrat party desperately try to lure people to vote for socialism.

Their perversity and lies and falsity are unimaginably high!

These are hard time for the Venezuelan people, no one of these democrats dare to criticize or public accuse the Maduro regime or to encourage the population to opposed to his oppressive regime!

As is not enough shame in Democrat's actions they started to silence about Venezuela Cuba regimes and step by step to unmask themselves as fanatics future socialist leaders of their spread socialism.

This is strong proof that Democrats really do not care about ordinary people, their sufferings and by contrary without any doubts they show the hope and desire to live in real paradise life having everything they want and to have right to dispose of everything like Stalin, Lenin, Ana Pauker, Maduro, Castro and Kim Jun Un and so on.

Just days before Alexandra on occasion told people that she invented the good idea of New Green Deal and the people have to work for her now because she is the boss!

And her desire to subjugate people is clearly evident! He started to abuse of everything exactly like the socialist leader Ana Pauker in socialist country.

I suggest to these democrats to live in Cuba for several months to see, to feel and to really understand how the socialist regime is!

Even the students to go to experience a socialist life. They cannot understand how it is to be hungry.

Now we the people understood perfect how false and dangerous they are!

And any politician who tries to propagate or spreads the greatness and the grandeur of socialism are for sure very sick, mentally handicapped, hates the people, and they need surely a person around for personal comfort and kind of balance.

These abnormal people must be separated from society and interned in special hospitals to give them special psychiatric treatment.

Look at *Monster Dwarf* Nadler and Schiff judicial members how red their eyes became so huge hatred in their faces put and so strange sound in their voices and how irregular move their arms when it comes to revenge for his party.

If the Democrats crazy hooligans are not sent very soon for mental treatment and reeducation, all planet will be in huge trouble!

If you like Orwell's *Animal Farm,* then you will soon be in socialism!

Lies cannot replace the truth and the human being needs truth even more than food or anything else.

Millions of victims of odious socialism are witness to that.

We cannot feed on empty words that socialism is different that the American socialism that the Liberals are itching to impose.

Just like the victorious socialism collapsed, so it will do in America.

At the first sight the socialism is against any human being. Why?

Probably Karl Marx hatred so much human being tricking them for an imaginary, fanciful, perfect, ideal, and bright society that 100 percent his theory will bring like gift to poor people!

Maybe some people wanted the socialist society but soon they realized that for very modest advantages like a modest house, a modest health insurance, free school and job, they really lost everything. Lost any kind of personal rights, no right to religion or free speech and you have to enjoy only the culture events approved by political regime, and to agree totally with what your great leaders said about everything because your opinion never will be heard.

Let us talk about this false "free" school.

In any Socialist country, school is free only until high school.

To start the high school, you have to take special test to be promoted.

If you do not pass these tests, you have no choice and have to go to vocational schools that do not meet your family expectations.

After high school, you have to take a very hard test to finish it.

To go to college or universities, that is another story.

To become a Doctor, Engineer, Lawyer, or Teacher, you have to take very selective exams and compete with thousands of other countries candidates with limited spaces.

The chances are very slim, and it is possible that you may never pass these difficult exams.

So your dream to be what you want is an illusion. Not to mention how many "powerful" candidates from special political areas will take your place in an unfair manner.

But in free countries you can achieve your dreams, even if you have to work for some money to pay school taxes. And a college or university in America will admit you as a student and limping hobbling along, your dream comes true. Only here in America is it possible. Not in Socialist countries. Capito? Miss. Shit Alexandra, stop lying!

In Socialist countries, you lose any kind of personal rights. No right to religion or free speech and you have to enjoy only the cultural events approved by political regime, and to agree totally with what your "great leaders" said about everything, because your opinion will never be heard.

Forget the right to free demonstration or free speech.

You have an absolute right to say "nothing". If you want to say something it is on your huge risk.

To become a political prisoner is very simple.

If a boss or one with huge power does not like you or wants your nice wife or house or car or so forth, over night the secret police will arrest you and will send you in the middle of the hell campuses.

After that you no longer count as a human being. See the novel *The Process,* by Kafka, a Jewish writer.

The special program to slowly exterminate you works very efficiently.

And slowly, from a very innocent man, you will admit strange deeds you never did, and to recognize you are a very, very bad person asking the torturer to execute you.

Because there is no legal justice or responsibility of care of you soon will die and no one will know about you.

The Socialist government created a special system so you will never disturb the Government with these "stupid" questions.

You have a sacred right to flatter, to oxlip, to praise, to fawn, to incense your leaders for everything they did or said. Otherwise, the Secret Service will disciplined you using the barbarian, bestial, criminal, inhuman, unbelievable to imagine methods in special secret campuses, from where usually no body never escape.

All days and nights the strong and permanent propaganda will keep busy your mind, dreams, ideas, and hopes, helping you to clear understand that you are living in paradise, and you did not realize it so well yet!

The general lack of most primary needs starting with food and any article for dress shoes or any other article of normal need as human being is hard very hard to find, or came too, too rarely in government stores and a very large corruption, immorality, and humiliation cover all level and structure of society.

Women are very much exploited and started to admit their immoral life to take pleasure in receiving any item or for a job, because at jobs there's no need to do anything than being the girlfriend of the boss.

Due to the general lack of almost anything of items from any story, the corruption cover all government buildings, or all hospitals, or any school, or any court and everything have a price, no way.

They respect your vacation but never ever in non socialist countries.

And any innocent contact with citizens from noncommunist countries is considered a treason act; you will pay hard for it.

And so easy to be declared a political enemy and next step a political prisoner!

A perfect isolation from these countries their news or culture and their citizen will be very strictly and total.

You are not a person just a number very much watched by Secret Service and your neighbors.

Your socialist country created the most possible bestial, criminal, abominable, cruel, inhuman, immoral, corrupt, terrorist, police regime.

In behalf of an unknown future but almost a paradise, full of happiness, equality, wealth, much-desired life they install very brutal, directly a dictatorial political regime, indented to crushed any slightest attempt to change something!

Even if you try to adjust your new life to this kind of society, the general panic, scariness, not to be arrested for any explanation really makes your life a hell!

But for everything in exchange you got the right to be totally silent and to suffer quietly!

Some people understood what about the socialism is but are too late.

Some tried to escape with their families but with supreme sacrifices.

Many official people decided to escape from this wonderful socialism. So diplomats, sportive, military without any doubt run away when they really have a small chance.

But it will bring a lot of misery and it's not worth experimenting with not even for a second.

For sure the socialist leaders make huge mocks about people for their vote, to get power what they really want forever and by all means!

In a socialist country, you will fast understand that no talking about rights and no chances to make more money than others, to dress different, or to dare to be different.

All resources are incredible limited and you have a new interesting job to fight for existence. What about Charles Darwin?

In socialism, the resources are very limited. But for Government officials, no problems. They have special stores, only for their access where they can buy all kinds of food, technical modern products, and everything that most others never dream of. And above all they use have and enjoy only the highest capitalist furniture, technical items, cosmetics, and everything they like, just for their pleasure, even if they blame totally the Capitalism system. Look at this animal dictator Kim Jong Un in North Korea who lives a dream life in his huge, large, and secret Palaces. But would never think twice, about killing his unsubordinated slave very fast.

Honestly Socialism establishes a very strong Slavery system.

A strong propaganda days and nights propagate the idea that any member in Socialist country has to make huge sacrifices to give up to anything for a golden Future for new generations! And people now have an ideal to love and be happy for their shit criminal life at least for the golden future of new generations!

Using all the time the false word *free,* for school, for transportation, for doctors, for houses, for food, for vacations, almost for everything is really a big-smelling, tricky lie.

No society in the world is ready to offer such only advantages.

Secondly this idea is very dangerous against all people.

The life is short, and we as human being needs the progress, independence, the strong desire to grow up to win any times to compete, to be the first to be active, to look for all kind of challenges, to have some personally for our soul, to be indivisible, to be different from any point of view, to go we think is proper for us! So we need to do something for our better and better existence.

If someone tries to give us all free, that is a big lie. What about my personal philosophy, about my contribution for my future, about my dignity?

Very wrong and a lie!

If some people have no jobs, then give them a nice and serious opportunity to find a proper job for them and train them in a special place to regain news skills, new knowledge, and pay them during this training period.

After this period of good time, he must be placed in proper working place, not to give them false illusions that all will be free.

Look how ridiculous Di Blasio looks offering all the time free services instead to give to people of what they really need jobs! Di Blasio just steals money from hardworking people to give to others. You know why?

Because a very interesting practice in the hand of so to say socialist leader the best practice all the time to use and work with others money people never to use a cent from their pockets!

—⚊—

The manner of punishing innocent people called them political prisoners for no real reason it is unique.

In Russia, Vladimir Ilici Lenin, known as the Little Man, organized a special perverse service, a kind of secret one, to hoax people that this is against the socialism and in very simple way found out everybody who decided to fight against socialism and to kill them in the egg.

He ordered to all members of Secret Service to make any crime against political prison so abominable so to be heard at a distance more than two hundred miles so people to be scared and frightened forever.

And a big political leader in Romania, a Jewish lady, came from Russia, Ana Pauker, who was working in a socialist committee party, used to bring political prisoners in her office and after putting their clothes out and tied their hands and legs by a furniture took a pen and started beating bestially over testicles till the poor man fainted by huge amount of pain.

Very excited Ana Pauker asked the guards to bring this faint victim to bathroom and to put them in a tub full with ice and water to recover. And very fast she ordered the guardians to bring the man almost dead back, and she continued more excitedly, torturing them for hours.

In Es Germany or in, Bulgaria, in Czechoslovakia, in Poland, and so on, all socialist countries the political prisoners were put out in the middle of a very harsh winter in the stark naked and for hours they were well wet with the hose and in the very warm summer they put the political prisoners in metal boxes very thick for hours without any drop of water.

The norms of work in campuses are intentionally made not to be possible to achieve. So the very sick, hungry, weak and fearful inmates now have to be punished in very barbarian ways. When they return to campus they have to stay on long, long, long rows to be bitten. In front of the door they have to be ready with pants down. Four guardians lay them on the cement floor and the other one started biting them with a criminal pleasure and after 25 lashes and crying with huge pain they wait out to be incarcerated in special cages. For 2–3 days without food or water, they have to stay only on legs in a very narrow cage. And after that to go to work again! And when they have once a year visiting hours, in a large room more than 25 political prison stay in front of their desperate families, parents and start to talk. A very deafening noise around because the relatives stay in front of them at a 10 m distance and each wants to find soothing about each other. The guardians walk around them and if something seems suspect, they order them to stop and after 2–3 minutes the visiting hours is closed.

In socialist countries no one care about ordinary people. They can be killed mutilated used for experiences or pure and simple to disappear forever.

In Cambodia, the big, loved supreme leader Pol Pot used to kill millions of political prisoners simple and chip and economically very efficient procedure he invented and being so proud of his invention.

Long lines of political prisoners were brought on the large stadium and behind them Secret Service members wait the beginning sign for mass killing.

When the great Pol Pot said now very fast, the Secret Service members ran behind each political prisoner and fast covered their head with a plastic bag. In couples of minutes, they died by suffocation, and the plastic bag were used for next political prisoner, and in two three hours all convicted people were dead.

And the fascination of discovering the power to inflict huge pain killing innocent people for imaginary reason or invented reason create a permanent desire to do it again and again and again.

Why not? No slightest track of justice or responsibility.

In this human socialist regime, they became overnight the god for all these innocent people that choose to live or forced to live in it.

The socialist political system imposed a group of selected people to keep the total power and to dispose of everybody or anything as they like.

The very well-known personal cult made strange mental sick or really idiots the genius ones, the son of the nation, the son of the earth, or the son of the universe, and in a very shameless, improper, incredibly exaggerate manner attributed them feature, qualities, exceptional power, perfect mind.

And days; and nights' radio, TV, press or huge panels in cities, or anywhere in the workplace to remind you you're so lucky, happy to have such a kind of leader!

And these strange families decide for your happiness to keep the power forever.

See North Korea and the huge suffering for millions of people that are so unlucky to live in.

The Secret Service has very discretional and total power so their brutal, abominable and ferocious behavior are intended to spread a permanent fear, horror, fright, and terror. Everyone will live in a terrifying atmosphere, feeling frightened out of their wits and paralyzed with fear.

This anecdote will express perfect the life they are living under Socialist philosophy created by Karl Marx.

Mr. John is coming from his job, looking to find something to eat and then watches TV. He goes to bed and after a couple of hours a very hard, deafening noise at his door made him wake up. Very frightened, he goes to answer the door. "Who is there so late?". The voice said, "The death! Your time is up!" Than Mr. John very happily, very relaxed, very calmly said, "Thanks my GOOD GOD! Thank you, thank you so much. Wow! I was so, so, so scared, my heart pounding to break my ears because I thought the secret service was here to arrest me."

—◦—

So for millions and millions of lost live in a very cruelty, abominably, criminally, inhumanly ways in short time in socialist countries and for huge sufferings and lack of normal life for others millions of innocent victims, I firmly ask international courts to convict the person named Karl Marx, born on May 5, 1818, in Germany Tier, from parents named Heinrich Marx, father, and Henriette Pressbur, mother, in a Jewish family to death, postmortem, and to the demolition of all his statues of course in the free world.

This sentence is just small part of what they need and desired in order to alleviate by 0.001 percent of sufferings the humiliations and the dishonored human beings that were brought under unimaginable tyranny!

Maybe Karl Marx was well intentioned and in honesty dreamed that this socialism is the best solution for millions of poor people, but unfortunately this man tricked himself and all the people who his allegedly tried to help, or Karl Marx really hated so much the human beings, doing everything to punish them in this bestial way!

However, the final results of his socialist philosophy shows without a doubt that its real results from socialism is a big ruin in all possible planes for humanity!

The sentence is needed due to his total lack of personal knowledge and education or studies, he, Karl Marx, never understood the profile, the structure, and the soul of human being treated them like a happy heard of irresponsible inferior animals that need desperately to be guided or leaded and to be happy having some to eat and personally to use.

This is totally false.

Human beings from the very early age prove a very strong desire to be independent, a winner, a leader to compete and to win to be unique all the times, to get respect and consideration, conquer new horizons to work hard, and to make a lots of money to indulge a nice happy without any needs lacks full life, to trip anywhere in the world and to scrutinize his environment with a unfinished interest and considering the most fundamental right in all his life the truth only the truth.

The human being needs the truth more than food or something else.

So to be clear, human being prefers to die for truth.

Any lie is unacceptable, special when it comes to his life, personal life to politics or his future.

He wants desperately to know he is crazy to know and the lie makes him a totally other human being, very unhappy and very sad and feeling so humiliated.

This International Court Convention to death postmortem of this man Karl Marx is symbolic.

But it is a modest attempt to pay an homage in the memory of so many innocent victims of this lie and strange and fantasy socialism. But the most important effect will be to stop Democrats partisans of Socialism anywhere to lie innocent people of how good or perfect and wonderful the Socialism will be for the American people and so, to stop shameful lying that in Socialism everything will be free, free, free, free!

Comrade Karl Marx, it's time finally to find out that any human being feels so humiliated when someone gives him free food, clothes, or pay him money for doing nothing.

He wants to have everything he wants and desires wealth, simple, real truth, but to work hard responsible in exchange for his wealth.

Contrary to your socialist theory is totally against those who want to work hard to achieve more.

Practically your theory, Comrade Karl Marx, punishes very much the hard workers the inventers and finally hated success.

God forbid to try to be a successful person, all government officials will think bad of you and will stop you and punish you.

Why? Because economically free people are not too obedient. The great genius leader expects from everybody.

Karl Marx was a very modest, so to say "philosopher"

He never created something original. NO!!!

He just fraudulently copied all ideas from others, such as Tomaso Campanella the "Walled City of the Sun", JJ Russo, "Social Contract' or Proudhon, Thomas More even from Bible and so forth.

Karl Marx with a little smacks of learning, had not enough power of mind to understand simples but FUNDAMENTAL principles of real life such, the personal wealth will be a good chance for a rich society or a very poor, or uneducated, or strange modest future leaders using his confusing philosophy about Socialism will become big, terrorist, criminal, and fast based on CULT of Personality will start thinking that they are the GOD of people and these bad leaders will do not respect any right, rule, law convention, tradition, religion, family, feeling and so forth.

Their instincts, desires, dreams, fantasys or imaginations or personal guts will be strongly imposed to ordinary people.

Karl Marx never saw the danger that in Socialism these new leaders will never respect a law.

THE LAWS will NEVER be respected by them!!!!

Why to respect the laws as long as they are the GODS of people!!!

And very soon and easy the new leaders created the most possible criminal, terrorist, abominable Secret Service with the total right of live or death over population!

Which will crush in egg, pitilessly, mercilessly any human being, who seems to be dangerous for them!

Intentionally the new leaders of Socialism develop a special Propaganda Department to keep the mind of every human being very busy and under permanent raping, abusing, violating the consciences. So from early age to the last days population were obliged under serious kind of punishment to attend after work, hours almost daily, long meetings in which debate the <great success of Socialism, to praise how great leaders they have> even if they do have nothing to eat, dress or to use. This bestial and permanent indoctrinating process, never finish, making the stress a very killing one. People are obliged to lie in everything. The radio, news papers, and TV just promote every moment the false news about the great leaders, life, happiness you are living in, and you did not see yet.

And a life of general fear, terror, desperation, lack of any needs for a common life is largely and totally installed.

So Karl Marx brought for many, many years huge amount of all kind of suffering over lots of populations because he was unable to see the huge real hide criminal potential in his filthy philosophy.

Very strange but in different countries, with different languages, culture, traditions, psychological factor, races, colors and so forth and very far away each other, the same Karl Marx, "so to say" "philosophy" brought the same, identical drama. genocide or human disaster!!!

And after many, many years of long suffering and a very, very long miserable life people decided, by any risk to throw away your BIG HOAX and Socialism collapsed in many countries.

The new propaganda big lie that <We have to sacrifice all now, for the GOLDEN FUTURE of new generation, proved to be another sham lie.>

Just China made huge changes. Smart new leader in China understood that your strange, stupid, inhuman philosophy does not work anymore and only reach people make a reach country.

They decided to change this shit political with new trends and to let people to make money, to invent, to create for them and society.

They understood fast that if people have more money the Government will have more money to invest in large public projects, eventually to help others!!!!

---

Why you Karl Marx did not bring goodwill, equality, total respect for the law and happiness for this human being??

If you should have brought wonderful real beautiful good life, sure I should have been the FIRST to fight to install such a great society!

But sorry, nothing of the kind!

Socialism was and it is a big, big hoax for people hopes!

You and we know now that, THIS KIND OF HOAX SOCIEATY IS NOT POSSIBLE TO EXISTS NO WHERE IN THE REAL WORLD!!!!.

Only on the paper or in sick mind, as your terrorist, criminal Karl Marx, so to say "philosopher "!!!

I see!

Because you hatred so much human being punished them so hard and made a criminal experiment over millions of innocent people!!!

Shame on you!!! You must be punished now!

And after so evident, clear, for anyone that Socialism is a big hoax, I expect you to be honest, to go out from your TOMB and take all document about your lie, hoax Socialism, and throw them in the GARBIGE CAN OF HUMAN HYSTORY, so never ever one single human being to ever see, hear or read them!

---

So, Karl Marx just read these others books and created a very fantasist, confused, irresponsible, terrorist so to say "philosophy", due to which millions, and millions and millions of innocent of man, women, children were died, mutilated, obliged to suffering hard to imagine humiliations or disappeared for ever over night.

His DIALECTIC, as a method of researching is a big FRAUD. The real genius German Philosopher EMANEL KANT is the inventor of DIALECTIC, it is true he used it in IDEALIST field.

But the three laws of DIALECTIC are unique in UNIVERS and these were discovered by this real scientist Emanuel Kant, never by Karl Marx. Period!

The strange idea that people must be equal economically is a bad fantasy, a huge mistake, so voila, the socialism collapses, and will collapse forever.

Sorry, comrade Karl Marx!
Try again never!

—⁂—

*Please, Americans, wake up!*

It's time to understand the perverse and imminent danger!

—⁂—

Entirely my life I asked myself why America is the dream of all human being on the earth and why all people of the world want and die to come and live here in USA.

America is a country where American Constitution is taken seriously and protected by Senate and Congress, and it is respected by each honest American citizen!

Only the human rights here are really protected and respected.

Here and only here the police protect and serve all American citizens!

And here only the law is for all and no one is over the law!

Then because is the country where the American Senate and American Congress are very, very concerned to develop a special agriculture capable to feed every day all his citizens, regardless if they work or not at all for this food!

Here the Americans, the president, the Senate, and the Congress are madly concerned that each American citizen never ever has to suffer for lack of food!

Thousands of social programs for helping all people in need or the donation system are generously created day by day and used daily to help all in need!

The hardworking people admit this financial effort and are proud they can do this!

Across history, many political systems failed in lots of countries, but never in America!

And never will fail as long as America means the world dream, even if some Democrats people hope to humiliate America to make America weak and ridiculous and small!

So start protecting America just from this moment!

—∞—

I come from France where the state is desperately trying to impose socialism with a humane face, but I think a new revolution will start.

Taking more and more money from the people who work and giving it for free to others is not going to be tolerated any longer!

"Bankruptcies in many fields and the imminent collapse of the French economy will lead to the end of the deceitful socialism!"

I remember that many Americans fought for this inhumane socialism in wars overseas.

One of them is di Blasio, who soon intends to candidate for the White House!

—∞—

Being sick and tired of lies, sufferings, starvation or the criminals' expressions "Nothing remains for you" or "It is finished" and understanding that the socialism hates and punishes very sever any form of zeal or personal initiative, people perfectly expressed all in one classic slogan.

"In socialism, all people are obliged to do all what they want to do!"

—∞—

I played some tennis

Roger is very good at tennis.

He won all sets.

Eugenie, his beautiful sister, smiled to me sweetly, and I was happy.

But she didn't talk to me or asked me anything.

She has got a very strong character.

She knows what she wants to do and doesn't deviate from her plans.

I swear I would really be happy if she was my girlfriend.

Time passed by just like it does day after day.

We parted ways and decided to meet again and talk and play tennis.

Before going, Roger called me, "Jimmy, when will I see you again?"

I was surprised, but I replied quickly, "Whenever you want! Give me call."

---

Roger called me after two weeks. He was a little agitated and asked me to meet him right now.

I said yes. And in couple of minutes, we met on our street.

Very fast, he confessed that he is very concerned with his family.

His father wrote a series of politic articles about real life in America.

He decided to publish them before meeting a lawyer. It is all right, and he legally could publish them.

But some interest groups could have very violent reactions and they could attack their family.

It is possible to beat his kids to kidnap them or to kill them easily.

They can take him from the street and execute him mafia style. All under special protection of those that are very interested.

"My father doesn't even have a gun, and he is not able to protect himself and his family. We his kids and mother are stressed of the death. After publishing the articles, we started receiving all kind of phone calls. During the night somebody started calling us but refused to talk at least two three times. They call during the day, but they speak a language that we do not understand.

"Daddy thought to call the police, but he is still undecided. He thinks that all members of our family must pay a hard price for his boldness to mix in American matters. Poor guy, he does not eat or sleep, and he is a walking corpse. Honestly he does not regret at all that he published these articles, but now he expected everything wrong.

"This is a matter of principle. He is good man and never ever he will do something wrong, but the justice is a hard problem for him. He is afraid for us his kids and mother, not for himself.

"Jimmy, I know you a very good colleague and very intelligent. I found it out by chance from many others students. I know you know the politics from all points of view. When I talked to you about my father and his articles, I remembered you did not say anything. You did not engage in dialog, just you listened.

"What do you think, is it something very bad in what I told you last time? It is possible to be punished for these published articles or they will let us alone?"

—⚜—

Jimmy looked at me and tried to smooth my agitation, but he didn't have power to convince me.

He was a little evasive and unclear.

I think he did not believe that in America such a thing was possible.

I think he was very scared something wrong might happen to us and was surprised and confused in what he said.

It is true if you come to America and subscribe to the Liberals, everything will be all right and nothing wrong will come to you.

The justice is the armed arm of Liberals, and they do all things now.

Suddenly Jimmy started to get very scared.

"Well! It is possible to kidnap Eugenie and to rape her or, worse, to kill her and no one can protect her. These things happen every day and not too many are punished for these kind of deeds."

Jimmy became desperate that Eugenie could be a victim and started speaking faster and faster.

He tried to find a solution, but only for Eugenie.

He really lost his mind. He forgot of me, my mother, and even my father. Only Eugenie was important for him now, and he tried desperately to know how to protect, save, or defend her!

He already saw only the bad in action and was very scared on how easy she could be kidnapped and abused by any animal from the street.

I tried again to bring him to earth.

A little embarrassed, he said that anyone from my family must be protected.

He became a little quiet and honestly looked for a solution to protect the entirely family.

But he did not find out any solution. It was very difficult to find out something good and for long time!

He promised that he will think about it and never will he give up.

I said, "It will be good to keep in touch from now on by phone or by direct observation."

We separated, more optimistic.

---

Not two days even passed, and Roger called me and very scared asked me, "Did you see the new traffic signs "No Entry" on our street?

An official car followed by two police cars have come on our street. The policemen stopped, and four big traffic signs were planted fast on our street! I asked a policeman which was in his police car. He told me clearly that the mayor ordered this action to help the thousands and thousands of professional revolutionaries which soon, very soon, will come to this area to picket our home as they did in front of the governor in Wisconsin and in Manhattan.

"So we expect these thousands of revolutionaries to come in front of our home with drums and to start drumming days and nights to scare us and tohorrify us. In this way, they will clearly express their democratic opposition against other political opinions, as the Constitution said.

"My father understood what will be and decided to exit in front of them with a special banner on what he will write.

"'Please shoot me! Leave my family alone to live normally! The published articles were written by me only! By me only!'

"I do not know what to do now. My family is very scared and understood that the thousands of revolutionaries which soon will occupy our street for many months will be violent and all are supported by officials. No one will try or can help us!"

Jimmy became perplexed.

This was too much for him who knew the American Constitution by heart, for his strong American education, and really was unable to say something!

He was so scared and said to run fast back to France before the professional revolutionaries would come to their street!

I never saw him so scared, and now he did not care even of Eugenie.

He thought with horror the huge social problems the published articles created even if they were legal!

He returned to his home without saying anything!

Now he clearly very clearly understood that some special groups could do all they want following the orders of people very up!

So the American Constitution is finally a big nothing for those that have political power!

# EPILOGUE

Many times, I meet people, places, situations, and all kind of events that remained in memory, but all the time asked me to tell them to others.

The silence disappears, and something hard to understand overwhelms you, assaults you, and pushes you not to keep silent.

Waiting to say to all who want to listen to you, your memory does not offer any place to hide or pretend that you can do everything you like.

Long time ago I did a pact never ever to think to them and even more to give up to such a thoughts and memories.

But not possible at all.

During the night or day, those rush over you, stop from everything you planned to do, and push you with strong force somewhere you can write.

Whatever you try to hide yourself, to avoid it, to pretend that you are not that one, or to run from its way, it is an delusive thought.

You must to listen to it, to follow it, and practically to obey to it.

And the thoughts become words, and the words start linking in propositions and page after page in a special amazing dance rush to an end of the book.

No way to oppose. The memory force is like a volcano.

It shakes you, burns you, and takes your peace and quite so dear one day.

And tired of this long and impetuous effort, there is no time or power to decide if is good or wrong.

Now the book it is here.

Sometime ago I did not have to care of it.

But I had to do it, and I did do it.

But the people for whom I wrote it are the ones that have the right to judge me only!

And is so easy to judge!

Author,<br>Puiu Ion Pavel

Life is unique. Everyone has a life for themselves. Many times, I met people, visited places, saw situations, or encountered lots of events that have remained in my memory at all times. Reading books from an early age, I discovered that this is the strong and sure way to real freedom!

Meeting all kinds of people, seeing with my mind's eyes their lives, and talking with them, I learned enormously.

Any human being has a special value when they do something to contribute to the progress of society by science or art or innovations or daily hard work!

So, all my life, I have worked very hard, and I educated my family in this way.

I was impressed and amazed at what human beings can do!

A long time ago in my early age, I wrote a poem for my mom that was published in a local newspaper.

I wrote two other books, but I never had the financial power to publish them.

Working in many fields of activity, I talked with people that told me very interesting things.

I understood very early that human beings deserved respect and consideration for doing something good for society.

What is good for society is good for themselves and their family, and this is important.

This book is like a flame in my soul.

I did all in my powerto publish it so that people can read it, of course the people who want it.

The book is an expression to help people to stay together.

Killing or stealing or hurting others must stop, by all means!

Life is a serious job. Everyone has a chance. But you are the one to make a choice. Always build, never demolish.

Finally, life puts everyone in the position he or she really deserves!

You have the right to criticize the book!

And it's so easy to judge.

Made in United States
Orlando, FL
30 August 2022